COINS IN RIVERS

Shortlisted for the 2019 Gaudy Boy Poetry Book Prize, New York

Longlisted for the 2019 Beverly Prize, UK

Rochelle Potkar is an alumna of Iowa's International Writing Program and was a Charles Wallace Writer's fellow, University of Stirling. Her poetry book *Paper Asylum* was shortlisted for the Rabindranath Tagore Literary Prize 2020 and her poetry film *Skirt* was showcased on Shonda Rhimes' Shondaland.

ALSO BY THE AUTHOR

POETRY

Four Degrees of Separation

Paper Asylum

The Coordinates of Us

FICTION

Bombay Hangovers

PRAISE FOR THE BOOK

Exceptional work, this. A haunting inventiveness runs through these poems. Rochelle Potkar's imagination is rich and carefully employed to her poetic purposes, sensitively met with through her concrete imagery and cosmopolitan vocabulary.

Jayanta Mahapatra, awarded the Sahitya Akademi award and the Padma Shri

These fierce, fearless new poems of Rochelle Potkar seem nothing less than a continent adrift, forging not only a new language, but a refuge from our present aesthetic dystopia.

Philip Schultz, Pulitzer Prize winner, and Founder and Director of The Writers Studio, New York

Exalted and visionary, Potkar brings neologism and the old word, especially dialect, into friction. These poems spark and spin with feminine energy and surreal thought, critical reflection, and restlessness. History is grounded in the demotic experience. Technology and science, and sexuality, provide a foundation, but this sensuous world, endangered, careens headlong into a post-everything future without losing touch with the more human and fragile aspects of the Ancient. This is dynamic risk taking poetry.

Adam Aitken, Australian poet, and winner of the 2021 Patrick White Award

Rochelle Potkar crafts poems situated in the local which have currency around the world. Her ear for the music of the English language is impeccable. In this book you can count on finding poems bristling with a fabulist's world-view, detailing the lives of imaginative, creative protagonists.

Patrick Cotter, judge at Gregory O' Donoghue International Poetry Competition, Ireland

Rochelle Potkar is a poet fully engaged in this world of sublime beauty and horror. Surrounded by fecundity, her poems witness greed, as often as human kindness, and the reader waits nervously for what she will reveal: *my heart is a bomb she writes* [...] *And we wait for it to explode.*

Sandra Alcosser, author of *Except by Nature* and *A Fish to Feed All Hunger*

Like a restorer who undertakes many hours of intensive labor bent over surfaces ravaged by time and circumstance, Rochelle Potkar attends to uncovering layers to bring the small but important details of what was submerged to the foreground again. [...] divining cups sit next to beer mugs in the bazaar, ancient instruments next to new music albums. The reader dives into words as thickets of green bamboo chiseled by rain, until she understands the message that it is possible to view those displaced as "fly[ing] into the night to become stars."

Luisa A. Igloria, author of *What is Left of Wings, I Ask* and *Ode to the Heart Smaller than a Pencil Eraser*

COINS IN RIVERS

poems

rochelle potkar

hachette INDIA

First published in 2024 by Hachette India
(Registered name: Hachette Book Publishing India Pvt. Ltd)
An Hachette UK company
www.hachetteindia.com

SRD

Inside illustrations by Pia Alizé Hazarika

ISBN 978-93-5731-497-8

Hachette Book Publishing India Pvt. Ltd
4th & 5th Floors, Corporate Centre,
Plot No. 94, Sector 44, Gurugram 122003, India

Typeset in Fournier MT Std 11.5/14.5
by R. Ajith Kumar, New Delhi

FSC
www.fsc.org
MIX
Paper | Supporting responsible forestry
FSC™ C043100

Printed and bound in India
by Manipal Technologies Limited

For keya
For poetry
For Mumbai

CONTENTS

COINS IN RIVERS

BANKNOTES

PREFACE

I often think of poetry as light and sound. We can't perceive all the light on the spectrum, nor hear all the sounds: infrasonic, ultrasonic. So too, not all art is within grasp, but over time it just might be within understanding – a sign of our evolution and tastes.

Time is the whetstone of art, and Poetry, to me, metamorphoses akin to a water cycle: a cloud here, a hurricane there; a molecule here, a glacier there.

In this book, I realized I followed a similar trajectory to my earlier poetry collections: concentric circles from within to without, from below to above...and beyond. Being a storyteller for the page and the screen has affected my approach. Though poetry might happen in one exhalation, mine is also shaped by person, place, and phenomena. Manglesh Dabral, the late legendary Hindi poet, once said to me that very few poets can weave stories into their poetry, and that I was one of them. I take it as a compliment that the two art forms I hold close to my heart have merged seamlessly.

Poetry itself was in a slippery relationship with me not so long ago, standing adamant at my intimate temple door like a dutiful daughter as I tended to the patriarchal son of fiction. Even if I might have wanted to leave her, she never left me. Like a river, like rain – I have now given in to the transience of existence through poetry – submerging sometimes, emerging sometimes.

The coins of wisdom here are wishful, playful, telling of the beginnings of new civilizations, two-faced (always!) with imprints of the hunter and the hunted, flipped in a bet, or to prove a point. *Chitt bhi apni, patt bhi apni* – you will find many such at the bottom of this well.

If Poetry is the morse code of the Universe transmitted telegraphically between two people, where its inception is its execution, I welcome you, dear friend and reader, to these little bolts of lightning, these wild animal scents from my wilderness.

first
mint

Bread

When the earth-diver plunges into a seabed of dough
in the artisanal bakery on the curve of a road
comes bread on palm, waiting for sun,
life-sustainer with sugar, starch, gluten

cosmogonic passovers from cast-iron skillets
azotized and hydro-carbonated
deities of crunchy outsides, moist insides
fermented by lactobacilli
entwined, croissant-like, maple syrup–blissed

drawn from ex nihilo in open-air bakeries
off additives of bran, rye, legume flour
with salt, this loaf is gazpacho and salmorejo
of hypnopompia

from within the void
life without *aysh* is without eigengrau
ceremonies of phantasmagoria
states of amorphousness – oral traditions of myth,

thoughts of divinity
baguette giving way to unity; challah to duality, brioche to
 trinity
bread from the progenitors of sourdough and yeast
passing through worlds – psychic before physical
sound and word, cracking of the Egg
of a life dreamt first.

Old soldiers, bankers, tailors
now grinding grain,
salt-rising, bacterial, cheese-flavored foam,
leavening hope, textured in sweet crust
against the crumbs and croutons of daily kneading

grain rupturing, harvest of coarse flour
stocked in stone-built scent of the walls
bonfires of cold hearths *roti, kapra, aur makaan*

between the crumpets and cupcakes
pretzels, pandesals, eucharistic
the first light of chimera, warm as broth
baptismal as sun-kissed barley and sedge

bread for the worm, bread for the fish
bread for the rabbit, bread for the civet.

private
wallet

Keyholes

We hide our wet lace behind a trellis of plants, our voices
 honeyed from jaded soap operas.
Our requiems are parties inside our heads, earphone to
 earphone.
Tolerance in the diorama of this rented place.
No door of solace or shame left open.
They will keep boyfriends. And.
They will come with trouble. And.
They will eat meat. And.

But sometimes we translate into vixens: late night – girls with
 eye masks,
returning on the stairs – *shush!* the landlord is insomniac
to stilettoes and side-slits of little black dresses,
books, menstrual cups, and spandex.
Who will take responsibility for them? And.

Emerald nights pass into agate mornings,
the sapphire of our head scarves and prayer mats
from insular to secular near our 2 by 2 boxes.
We curl each night against thoughts of saffron eyes, bloodshot.

If the nights fall over our skin, our bodies become bottles
of wine, with a crack against it. Dripping… dripping…
They will get raped. And.

Wooden cages with wooden birds flapping to horizons,
we scrape air like parchment,
peeling secrets from walls of adopted jailhouses.
They will grow wings. And.

Serpentine winds belching histories of women
who left when they heard the bricks squeaking,
Shush! And not again! And please behave yourselves.

But we play safe in dog-chewed *chappals*, our cycle tyres
gripping
the road's ruggedness
as alleyways sugar-lip the broken sky
of old whispering neighbors.

All this for only one proper peg to place the key
of our russet city–freedoms.
They will wear short skirts. And.

In That Land under the Sun

In that land under the sun, where dry heat hits bone
and in your pocket you keep a red onion
to peel flakes at 46-degrees centigrade,
male poets speak of Kamala Das and her feminist poetry,

entering a friend's wife's kitchen
and directing her to abandon her breakfast preparations.
They are getting late. There are no cafes in the neighborhood,
yet they depart with a caravan of 15 ravenous townspeople.

Under an angry sun, hunger hitting inside their guts,
Pied Pipers talk of timeliness, reaching a nowhere-wilderness,

while the woman in her four-walled, steeled cliché
keeps away a mountain of grated coconut over flattened rice,
sugar, coffee, and unused milk, par-boiled.
Her father was a village radical... but she tucks her wet sighs
at the edge of her sari.

As onions shrivel in our pockets with intense upheaval,
men use Urdu and Marathi verses to fight God

and the women can't even fight the men,
who are not their husbands
because they know no poetry.

The Girl from Lal Bazaar

The girl from Lal Bazaar
sips divination off cups,
laced in ginger over a saucer of zodiac signs
in dark-dusky mornings after wine sediments in beer mugs
of last evenings,

gorging eyes off popped cardamoms –
brittle bones of promises,
unspooling the wedge of her mother's sari under umbilical,
swallowing the rain in vertical pills,
a land-locked dream gathers vapor,
through the thick glass of a *cutting-chai*
for storms in teacups.

As Chinese lanterns blow, she predicts smaller surfaces
for her future without straining dregs
that stir the night to cinnamon kisses,
like stars smudging daylight.
In maps of doubt, enmity, falsehood,
spade-shapes of fortune, mountains of hindrance,
patterns in camels, dogs/letters in heart, and a ring.

She starts at the rim like the white women did (after
independence),
holding teacup handles to their spiral bottoms,
reverse-imaging white-negative spaces in clumps of flavor,
breaking potencies of freedom – on a stain with satin.

The girls were then from Europa, Nippon, for the English
soldiers.
Now Madama drinks brew through her yellowing teeth,
stalking the labyrinth of dark snakes in hot water
from a kettle by the pimp,
bittering in tea-garden time – one hour ahead of the zeitgeist
present.

What's left is 14 lanes of women of Nepalese and Indian origin
in the old brewing market of flavors,
and she, the daughter of a *randi* who is into
the beatings of drums – even has a new track for an
international album.

She won't let ripples in the saucer of lip-smacking liquid,
quivering with delight, decide her near and far futures
in scaffoldings of condoms and collarbone-consciences.

Willow Witching

In heat spell before ground swell,
trembling, a woman goes pillar to post
for horse-trots of drops that spell likes robbers.
Dust flying mildew against her veins, surging in damp linen,
like dermis of wet mongrels.

For the volley on asbestos.
"We'll find someplace good."
Divination in gemstones and a witching rod.
Like the old rain man dowsing a hazel twig,
in the land of the *babu*'s office.

She runs around the whole bureaucratic system.
Like rain off slopes to cradle water
from flooded forests, water-boxing, pinning storms,
desalinizing brackish with layers of mud, at the very bottom.
Or importing by boat from rivers. (Ponds are goddesses.)

Rooftop proofing is her watershed moment,
plumbing, cisterns seizing water like wild tigers
for plants,
irrigation,
the laundry.

See the rain man too condenses fog, dew
while waiting for long-buried wells.

She now runs in the direction of a tsunami...
a river never reversing –
ridges to trap, crops to grow –
the parched becoming quenched.

She draws groundwater over glacial melts,
red-tapeism,
free of sediment.

Her hair open like a tidal wave. The rain on rhythm
in sodden paper boats, smiling at her reflection
in detention basins.

Rain against its own skin
– the world reopening,
skies re-beginning.

Oasis of home.

Amber

Still on deck with a few people…
The last boats have left. We are sinking…
The end is near. Some men are praying…

Searching for the oldest messages in bottles, even after
132 years
in ginger ale, holy water,
she is eavesdropping centuries of love, luck, friendships,
pursuing his favorite beer can, guy ropes off his beach tent.
She once drank the moon with him
champagne upon champagne, thrown to brine.
That perfection so true, it had to end.

Head bowed, she chances upon false eyelashes,
bottle openers, wave-smoothened pebbles,
wreckage to the weight of sand, shore stones.
And walking near Hamburg pockets a stone
that upon drying, ignites in her coat
setting ablaze memories off postcards.

Passers-by, firefighters come to extinguish
phosphorus from a WWII incendiary apparatus,
unstable after 65 years – missing chunk,
decaying like pain into her breath, gasps of air,
tremors: 4.5 on Richter scale,
entering soil, groundwater – a man-made volcano,
too cold for revenge, too old for regret.

As when he left her like evacuating hundreds
in a child's play of *fire, fire on the mountain,*
in the sky, upon the earth, upon the whole, whole freaking-fucking-
frigging globe.

Three Women on Liberty Bridge

As the light dims, travel stills,
the bridge aligns itself to darkness,
we talk of the unveiling
of the Statue of Liberty...
(also, because she wasn't *desi*),

after the Communist regime
India, Columbia, Hungary...
through seasons of Satyugs 'n Kalyugs
of socialism, dictatorship, democracy.

We speak of womanhood
as lovers ahead, deluded by time
track the sunset, moonrise, clasping steel locks
with promises whispered over iron railings,

the stars slipping like rings around their irises,
the wind blowing urgencies over the Budapest river
rippling the mirage of the parliamentarian building.

And tearing the jugular vein of centuries, we hear
all the statues
were uprooted
from their old stumps
made to stand near each other
in Statue Park,

where they are still sparring
over their beliefs
in a crossfire
under the frozen eggs of civilization.

The Ice Factory

The ice factory owner Sarosh is a Parsi;
of a diminishing Indian community.
His voice so husky, like saw
scrapping ice to slush.
The factory produces ice slabs, ice cubes, ice blocks
to keep fresh soups, drinks, juice.

Sarosh visits on rare occasions, when
his phone rings, when glaciers are to melt
in sheepish Kalyan. Time moving backward.
No industries, agriculture in this town,
just a train junction, stopover for two historical sites: fort and marshland.

Today he receives a call at 8, to keep aside a slab, coming by one of his trucks.
He holds a jute-sack blanket
and before anyone else sees, his mouth goes agape,
a frozen woman – mouth ajar, eyes wide, hair far-reaching as capillaries, thighs
marked in red branches – tree to roots
is in a slab,
preserved
like in ice age.

She doesn't seem local – fair skinned in a red blouse,
skin olive, porcelain goddess... caught in surprise
of a photoflash with metal, mental, gun-dust.

The instruction is to ship her
with other consignments: flake, tube, slurry.

Between ammonia gas, gushes of water, common salt,
engines of electricity, hums of tanks,
Sarosh hefts the slab. Drives the truck himself.

A quick exchange at the landing sites. Flesh for fresh.
Fishing harbor sites of aquaculture.
This unknown woman is unnamed too for now,
before the search from her visa-country begins...
many unknown women-hunts
for lust, prize, or game,

who have gone through slabs to the Arabian Sea,
until time preserves the melt of truth,

each second – a loud plop.

Spring, Again

Ten days to mourn a father's end
in a lawless land.
She stands graduated, over soil pit
before a sick industrial unit.
Debtors, laborers like apparitions
come for wages.

Run, run away, they said,
nothing is to come of this.

She waits to splinter her body
against the wave,
sinking feet deeper in soil.
The seeds that sprout,
in sesame, sorghum, maize
before spring
impinge the grit
of her half-born sisters
in memories of
half-grown skeletons,
hemorrhaging cartilage.

Forget the turn of years in hours,
remember the color of the sky,
smell of pollen.

In a spare-parts locomotion production unit,
surgeries upon heart surgeries take place
for one more day of labor, of grace.

Finding winters in spendthrift summers,
washing debts, breathing easy.

Keeping planets in place
with an invisible hand
is art for well-oiled machinery.

The winds whisper of storms, songs
as she turns the clock back on tide –
inexorable deluge:
footprints and fingermarks,
guided alive by
long-dead roses.

Not Quite

At the outskirts of London with her blue-eyed brother
she asked what stuck in her dreadlocks.
Whom should she call father?
The one dying now of cancer –
for a DNA sample?

Casting shadows over terminal realities
unwrapping family history–trees
no word like black in her –
ebony skin of an ancient African.

Rage hurtles through her veins
like ancient coastal immigrants
between the tug of inexplicability,
genetic throwback or a Pakistani
Jamaican? Ethiopian?
Swapped at birth? Or adopted?

She never dated a black man or was seen
in the company of dark girls.
Even if her skin did not burn at 30°C.
She wasn't the smudge of sandcastles.
Even if you traced her to the 10th century.

Limerick nightclub of her mother's one-night stand
is a social construct.

Identity is a soul song
not a life-long legacy of melanin
pigmentation in unchecked checkboxes
of *preferring not to say*,
because *it's none of their business.*

Sight is more than reasoning –
sounds in perfect English
the speed of thought light-like
steeped with bigotry.

And talking telescopically…
her grandmother, uncles and aunties
wondered but never asked
on Sundays
of roast beef and Yorkshire puddings

because their love got in the way
of tiny microaggressions.

Prey

When the girl of 13 got obsessed
with the perfume of victory,
she waited outside an eagle's nest
before its chicklet flew
into the daring empyrean.

Her imagination etched against
barb-wired flesh wounds in a family of nomads,
where only men, for generations, hunted eagles
– the parade of sameness against the triumph of doyenne.

She now stands atop an unsound mountain
training her golden eaglet for the Ulgii festival
to the tremulous gasps of traditions.

And after the breaking of records, winning of competitions,
travels with her father into Mongolia's harsh winter for her
eaglet
to kill its first fox,
so they can all return like raven, rocky mountains against
the amaranthine skyline seen after a deep night's dream.

#MeToo Movement in India – Size Card

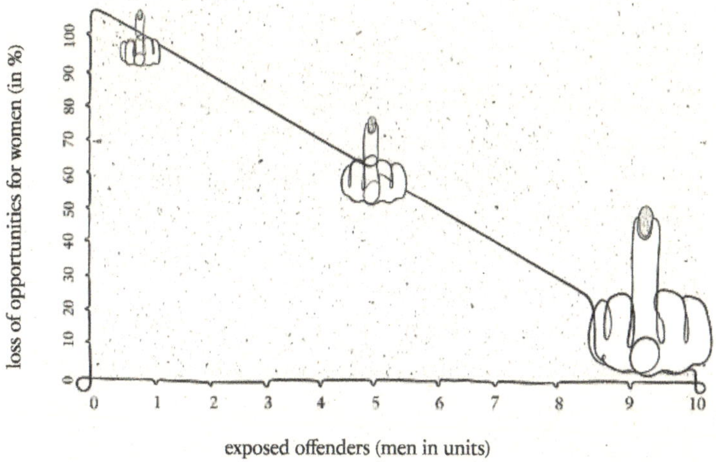

Sew

Khairlanji. The darkness of humanity percolates into corners over the skins of the mother and her daughter, those sons, the father. The darkness of the witching hour. Indigestible truths consumed in brittle cognizance.

When history has reasons, explanations for genocidal waves,
blind rage of the immeasurable...
appropriations of pain, Khairlanji can be explained away,
reasoned with, rationalized. Like the light kissing the cheeks
of another morning of other lives – when we held cappuccino
cups and beheld the sun smelt into a wealthy smile.
The Ferris wheel of souls.

Khairlanji: Casablanca. Hathras: Havana.

One life asking questions: the other answering it. If all lives were a tale of anguish between their acts, which is the life to feel the light? Which life is an interval over anguished skin? A caesurae or brink?

Water wheel: the stops at those stations, where electricity hasn't reached. Auschwitz.

One life in Hathras. The other thinking of it.

compost, last stage —
darning the patchwork
to the zillionth hour

Gravity

Transcendence
Self-actualization
Aesthetic needs
Cognitive needs
Self-esteem needs
Belonging needs
Safety needs
Physiological needs
A
B
C

antique currency

Anthill

No one could build or architect one.
Ants are not easy listeners.

They are migrants, militants
why would they come to give us lessons
in community building, strategy, or order
even if we don't have much?
Even for the food they steal?

It's a unique gift no one gave no one.
The most they gifted was a virgin island.

But I want you to have an anthill –
one that can be placed under your tree poems
where wise red-rich ants
organize their evolution, egg-laying queens
workers, soldiers, new nests,
nuptial fights…

(The Mercedes you can buy for yourself.
Someone can gift you a Harley-Davidson.)

I saw anthills in Matheran on
red clay trips made from childhood to
a second childhood (in adulthood).

They stood proud, the test of rain
their citadel – a sun-burnished

fortress of pride, of
underground passages,
no-aggression super colonies

and if you went close, they
attacked with pungent defense.

How would we migrate an anthill to your garden and house
then?
Will they listen to your poems?
Obey the winds?
Learn a new song?

The real purpose of an anthill home, is so we can
tame these organized creatures
tame unruly elements of nature –
all that an anthill was made of
strategy, order,
piles of earth, sand, pine needles,
clay, urine, and manure.

Surrender

If I were a country, you would be a journalist
and because you are not an
empty-headed bloke out for a quick fix
but investigative, committed, idealist,
I would have shot you down a street
and left you to bleed.

If I were a country and you my journalist
it would be a civil war, one too many
revolutions –
changes in governments.
I would have jailed you
and kept you under CCTV.

If I were a country and you my journalist
I would have played a wait-and-watch game
to see who wears the other
sleep-deprived akin to a Russian sleep experiment.

But the more you stare, the more beautiful someone becomes,
remember?

Many passed the cellars of my mind
few, the cellars of my heart.

I would blink first.

I would give in
from dictatorship to democracy.

If I were a country and you my journalist
I would let you run a free press and media

to change the face of an
entire nation.

Unreliable Narration

Sometimes I feel like that prisoner who has been so extradited, transported prison to prison, that he doesn't challenge the felony of fate, doesn't think of family and children, just goes into a tangential recovery of time, a z-axis of query. He goes and joins the citizenship of dreams, he follows the traffic lights of light banter, tipping the waiter the rightly recognized change.

He doesn't wait to return and when the shutters of his freedom scroll open, he is not thinking of something he never lost, but what he will lose now. The ability to be permanently lost. Now he will be found in the threads of the past pulled to make the present look woven, with continuity.

I realize all are everyone's lovers. An orgy of the world in eyes that watch, suspect, judge, appreciate, greet, smile. There are a thousand ways of lovemaking, that's why the world sustains, bomb after genocide after tsunami after meteorite, because people smile diffusing nuclear energy. Fissions of the heart. Fusions of desire.

He returns and his home was a foreign corner and every street had a name and hence unrecognizable and people had roles of wife, daughter, brother, uncle and couldn't be made sense of.

In Iowa there are proverbs engraved on manholes. What would a manual scavenger find there, I wonder? A language gurgling gutter. Secret files of sewage, the fecal waste of imagination, the pee and poo of amateurish essays. Story worlds that stayed static or antagonists that were too sweet?

Fireflies acquire the essence of moths burning to soot in their own arse-fires.
The burnt arses spot the sky like night galaxies of stories burning to be told, quivering to awaken. The prisoner in the unknown land can join dots on these constellations. Only he. You need an illiterate to read an unknown language and profess its translations into further more unknown languages.

burnt library –
upside-down alphabets
of banned books

The stoic pretension of decorum helps when planes are delayed. Bad weather. For once, it is the sky that throws tantrums and man listens. He and she sit waiting for revenge. Gaseous fuel combusting into the expanding space of the ozone layer. The sky does her hiccups in storms, songs in tornadoes, burps in hail, orgasms in hurricanes, salt-water gargles into gray.
On the other hand is the efficiency of raising voices in anger, yelling at the untoward weather, what men in India do when planes don't take off because of rapid desert dust storms. Our tantrums bigger than nature's.

We come first. No signals, lines, queues.
Even that doesn't help. Stoic or spontaneous. The best reaction has always been salted packets of humor, peals of laughter,

packaged bottles of irony. And if nothing, the dessert cups of lovemaking.

Lovemaking ends all of nature's evils. Procreation attacking creation. It puts nature in her place. Nature loves to listen to human orgasms, the same rumble of skies in the lowest decibel.

Lava

The body detonates long before it does. Like motherhood happens when you think of child, and love when you yearn before the lover crosses the crosshair of sight.
My body is bending at its curves, molten in a smelting ring. Each cell detonating where you last touched it. Old cells, as they go, are telling new ones of the way you will touch me in rough love, seeking old diary pages of a new broken song. A stanza forever eluding, the tune elongating, overlapped.
My body is receiving her swell and blossom, she is awakening in a thousand breaths.
All are letters, scent-kissed.
Just the mere thought of you is a thunder trapped in the solar plexus.
States of privilege are the states of being loved.
Immigration is home.
Your body is my home.
Your lips, my envelope.

Letters are teeth.
The messages of souls.

My body is awakening like a river under rain, torrid.
The woman awakening in the woman in the jungle.

After this comes Amazon, Athena, Venus.
My body is molting to the magma of breath. The silence that holds the worlds of longing.

Rehashed Mosaic

Should I send you a dream because
all words
have offloaded from the last freight truck…?

A dream that jumps the earth's technicolor palette,
borrowing mixtures from galaxies of pixelated pigments
via the Universe – your postman?

A murmur through the sheets of time bending like space over
    the centrifugal force of our kisses,
your tongue probing my mouth in an inter-galactic accident of
    mangled stars?

Our bodies aligned like a goods train, first train on track, a
    railway of dreams
gaze interlocking, breath interlocking, desire interlocking
as I bathe in your sweat?

Do you know how it feels under the canopy of your
    embroidered chest?
Your words both knife and salve.
Your words: gods, the elements, the stars who came down
to read the hieroglyphics created of them –
paintings on cave walls,
so life could come full circle, complete an orbit?

Should I send you a dream on the sleep of paper
of your intense gaze, the kindness of your smile, the generosity
    of your laughter,

my mouthfuls of your ear lobes – all the bread I could ever eat,
your undiscovered skin-territories like undiscovered truths
waiting for my nose tip for eons?

Skipping to the beat of your voice wrapped over gentle
    approximations:
of love, a movie, an idea, a story or a new daydream –
a new room carved for another soon-day?

The way I have loved you is the symphony of my eardrums for
the *bira* of your being – a concoction of presence
un-clipped toenails: a work-in-progress
not because I had the stamina, as much as you the potential.

You will know only someday of a woman deeply in love
like a diary found in a landfill
in post-apocalyptic utopia.

But tell me – do I send you a dream?

Rape Fantasies

Rape fantasies
by a woman are
seduction
rapeplay.

She dreams of being forced into
a sublime shift

intoxicated by drugs, semi-consciousness
coerced against the bulwark of will

knees crumbling
for the dangerous man
who must have her
like chocolate in a summer's palm

her body: her choice of self-betrayal
flagellation

cunt the
shape of an oyster, strawberry, rock sculpture
conch shell, flower with petals
pecan nut

the woman, dogmatic,
awaiting hurt

as she mows the lawn,
erects fences,
ploughs fields,
swerves plane,

speeds up jeeps,
steers the deal
brings the nation to its keel

and 'he couldn't resist her'
rugged warrior tamed through the pathways of
wet brute
an equality of imagination

contract of fantasy
over the consent
of reality

strong arms
giving in to the dirty game
in cusps and gasps
feigned struggle
of willing flexing ripples

even then
her greed for orgasms
choreography of sighs

pleasure beyond manners
forceful restraint

the ravages of
bodice rippers, shirtless men.

But
rape fantasies by men:
brutality

this gray is always difficult
to understand.

10 Things I Want to Do to You

I want to:

1.
take your ears into my palms
whisper prayers so they *shankh*-echo in the universe
like a fetal heart.

2.
hiss-whisper my tongue
over your nipples so they turn forbidden.

3.
wide-angle your thighs
like da Vinci's Vitruvian Man of math
to know the coördinates of your desire.

4.
suck your lips out
like a black hole in a load-shedding village
of burnt bulbs.

5.
rim your navel
so your solar plexus awakens –
axis mundi to star-dreams
where gazing is not myopic.

6.
nibble the vertebrae on your spine
see the calcified fossil of your character –
sediments of battles and bullets
the wars you have won.

7.
dislocate your knees
so when you venerate
fall to the ground
you are at once martyr, at once militant
patriot, at once nationalist
character and caricature.

8.
suck in your tongue, phallus
eat your fire
wicked sensing after theatrical niceties
so you can grunt like a goods-train
on alternate energy.

9.
suck your toes
my *sajda,* repentance
breaking down the temple of my body
toenails ripping taste buds
footsteps of a guttural hurricane.

10.
weave your fingers into mine
so the braille we are reading is no different
from the biometrics of unity

I want to meet the city of your body, its streets, its salons
underground networks of hope
play areas, dual zones
battlegrounds of despair
babies left in cots or
floating river-corpses.

Lastly, I want to:
kiss the arches of your feet
locate your Achilles' heel
the varicose of your journey
rumble of a hero's arrival –

left-foot *tandav* of ideology
right-foot ballet of universal manifestoes.

casino tokens

Harry Mendonsa

Harry Mendonsa, (may his tribe decrease!)
died on a vacation in Siliguri
at 98
on 27th January 2018, quite unexpectedly.

He, the consumer of Amul butter, Limca, Lipton tea,
lover of Krackjack biscuits, Gold Spot, Parle-G,
and Old Monk and Bagpiper on Christmas eves.

They found in his side cupboard
20 styles of brooms,
four harps, five mouth organs,
a sauce bottle that had turned black,
items from the flea markets,
and a bag of chips from 1976.

Anyway...
He was the user of Old Spice, Colgate-Palmolive, Dettol,
Amrutanjan balm, Borosil for burns, Dabur talcum powder,
and Gillette shaving cream.

They found under his mattress
a diary of how he killed neighborhood dogs,
polaroids and drawings of torture of birds and cats.
Some occult diagrammatic stuff...

Anyhow…
He is survived by his son Roger, daughter Alva,
grandchild Jane, wife Olga,
predeceased by brother John, father James, mother Jean.

Roger discovered letters with revealing photos
of several women.
Unopened, unused gifts atop his cupboard,
a box of sardonic emails for all the neighbors.
A gift to be opened only after his death:
of a cock ring, massage oils, and vibrator.

Anyhow…
He was a wearer of Bombay Dyeing, Bata *chappal*s, Raymond.
Purchaser of Reynolds pens, Bajaj scooter, Gold Flake.
Was always thrilled to travel Air India or on his Hero Cycle.
The last one to sip McDowell's No.1 on any child's christening.

His daughter Alva found divorce papers
from a previous marriage.
She never knew he was married before.
Also, a will where he left his garden spade
for her mother-in-law.

Anyway…
Harry was born in Naigon on Jan 8, 1920. A graduate of St. Agnel's Institute of Polytechnics.
Assistant manager at Ashok Leyland.
On June 2, 1945 he married Olga – librarian and school sweetheart.
On Dec 11, 1949 they welcomed Roger. He had five LIC policies

and loved Doordarshan on Onida TV.
He enjoyed carrom and travelling to 33 villages.
Problem-solver, he was in-house mason,
taking up difficult projects for his neighbors.

Wife Olga found condoms of different colors
in his drawers.
Porn magazines in attic boxes and
banks, names in anagrams with PINs
which turned out to be
women's names and phone numbers.
A briefcase with VHS porn
and lots of blue prescription pills.

Anyway…
An amateur badminton player at the Dombivli Sports Club,
he was into church activities, playing the mandolin at Saturday
services.
Every Sunday he ate at Saravana Bhavan or Murugan Idli
driving slow in his Fiat 1100,
sipping Campa Cola or Duke's Mangola.

A co-worker brought home his membership cards
to a sex club
and subscriptions to several sexual magazines.

His last words were: "I'm going to beat this, this is nothing. I
got away with murder."

Anyway…

He will be deeply missed by friends and family. A funeral service is scheduled for 1 p.m. on February 12th at Bardez Church, Karnik street. Reverend William Athaide will officiate.

Flowers, donations, condolences may be offered
at 23rd room, first floor, St. Joseph's Colony.

Bedding Day

When Santosh wanted urgent love marriage
in just 15 days,
he said, 'I need girl only for me
she has faith fully for me.'

He looked for simple things:
she should be a non-Facebook user, exceptionally fair
convented, at least Matric and virgin
or issueless and innocent divorcee,

completely non-feminist but an extremist
and compassionate, patriotic to country
with a keen desire to increase India's military
and sports capabilities,
expert in child-raising,
H1-visa no bar,
powerful and rich.

And congrations! He found her.
Her good name Priya
from top cawlej, tonty-two or tonty-one
with a dowry of ten thousant dollas.

They went for a spesal wedding party
with all drinks included: wiskee, vadka, jin,
child beer, strong rum than Old Munk.

The marriage hall
with unisex laboratories (for all those gay people)
was near Sharma sweets and snakes
rightside to Anus English Academy runned by Anu Sharma
in front of Santosh Tailors – Alteration of Ladies and Gents
and Welcome Turist office of 'We Spik Inglish'

at the backside gate, visitors were welcome,
only regrets to their vehicles
and no encouragement of baggers.

In Trust we God.
Santosh wetted Priya.
'They look like hiro and heron with their crowns no,' said all.
'They are laughing so much, showing
their Colgate teeth. In such atypa marriage
Go Slow – this is accident porn area,' said an uncle.

The gifts were many – bed shits and sony erection phones,
organic ghee from tension-free cows,
and kundoams in all flavors
like hot air balloons.

The only bilens were the in-laws
who took up the best gifts in compensasun.

'Shoplifters will be prostituted,' said Santosh
making his big red eyes.
But who were listening?
All mails and femails were busy
eating and drinking.

'Only their dead bodies will walk home,' he roared,
'neither on foot or ambulance.
Don't these peoples know I am yeS for Santosh – satisfaction
guarantee!
above all vermins and mens?
Get my spechal why-ta-mins
I want two children – both men.
yex, yem, yel, yen, zen!'

ATS

They never disagreed – Ruby, Tessa, Helium;
he didn't need coping mechanisms.
He sowed his oats into soft burgundy strands
or in the blonde, or the one with rolling blue eyes.
Each time he came life-size: wife, girlfriend, wife,
or slave, slut, whore
haunted by the happenings in Syria, or the price of potatoes.

He had picked them from inventors in a garage
teasing each lump,
picking each pinch of nipple,
flex of vagina, shape of breast,
quantum of lip,
succulent pulp, flexi-waist,
programmed orgasms.

> Somewhere they spoke of marriages
> society, safety and children.
> Not sex three times.

The blonde knew how to shudder
the brunette to surrender,
blue-eyes loved rape.

> Somewhere far a researcher
> was doing the rounds
> on new doll-makers and owners in town,
> dipstick analysis on loneliness,
> flaccid alienation,
> affinity to moist silicon,

as he celebrated triple birthdays:
he took them to the movies, grocery shopping.
Front seat of the car
turn by turn – with no insecurity,
emotional-redundancy.

Until the lamps went dry,
outside his smoky window.

They said of every innovation
colas and bulbs,
that in the first year
they only had early adopters,

You see, this was going to be one big – one BIG trend,
he thought quaveringly.

Litter of Applicasun to Eschool Principl

Loving sir,
My son, Premnath, 6th B, is the star of my eyes. We got
    invitation to Korepati show on TV. Come bull, beat me.
His face is going down when his mother say he can't come and
    wait for exams,
or else he dance to her expressions.
His mind is eating grass, a curtain fall over his mind. The
    matter has become tight in our homes.

His mother is making food in steel tiffins. Our first flight.

If I win this lottery even with slowest finger first, I will make
    your mouth sweet.
All five fingers in ghee. In our breaths come breaths.
But please let my son waste exam for show.
His mother made him hear ripe and raw.
I make one my sweat and blood.

Saved money for new clothes by each inch of my hair.
    Rickshaw driver, I see whole city – Bandra to Bhayandar.
'Go back to Bihar' they said. The city played over our lives. In
    our stomachs are always jumping rats.
We will give answer now of bricks with stones. In the dark
    night four days of moon.

I sell milk first but now it is in cold boxes in shops. Milk to
    milk, water to water.
The house cock is in the dal. Something's black in the dal.
Some part of my brain go lose. So three-wheelers.

He will study hard once coming back. God promise. Double in
night, four times in day.
We don't let him cut our nose, water sprinkling over our hopes.
Our respect shouldn't be removed or get lost in the mud.
His mother will eat him alive. We will color him in our own
colors or
the Ganga will flow in U-turn,
and I will make the donkey my father.

Once we win the karoad – one pomegranate, hundreds sick.
For the neighbors – may worms fall into their mouths.
Staying in the pond and fighting with crocodiles.
Going to sea and returning thirsty. But my heart first is
becoming a balloon.
Hope your school has night Inglish eschool for wibe-wa and
me.

This life is hard. A milky cow's kick we have to bear. Brinjal on
my plate. This hand give, that hand take.
On each grain is written the eater's name. Luck is a guest only
for four-five days.

Thank you, sir, for your parmissun.

Your loving,
Shanku Ram Murari

Frog, *postmoderne*

Of primordial legacies
as old as myoclonic jerks, dusk fears,
in our bodies, the dread is memories.

In a post-modern tale, the
innate fear of the frog is not of reptiles,
imprints from primate ancestors… as much as
hunted by the witch of society.
For mental disorders, foreign fads,

our frog has to come out again and again,
so he goes back again and again
into the bedroom of the princess.

The concern not of extinction,
mutilation, immobilization
… at the edge of the pond,
he always made razor-sharp decisions,

but the scare of separation
identity crisis of a hidden prince

a curse longer than three nights
loss of self, abandonment
humiliation, shame…
and the wizard's ways of keeping names.

Our frog has no gay icon
for a lover's kiss
so many cannot turn prince,
caught with another frog in bed
through the princesses' spy cam.

Drop a ball into this pond
the princess kisses the unwilling frog.

The dread of disintegration, and in another version
the frog is thrown against a wall to break the spell,
and in yet another – a Russian one:
Prince Ivan Tsarevich discovers a female frog
who comes out again and again
to become Vasilisa the Wise, female sorceress.

In modern tales,
the staying in is more important
with phobias of persecution, discrimination,
repercussions, violence

not ancestors' inheritance, whose love did not ensnare
the mesh of bodies to form other meshes
disrepair… despair.

In his pond,
the frog catches a reflection
of gods making love – fire and moon – Agni and Soma,
and Kaartikeya born of Shiva and Agni,

Mitra and Varuna, waxing and waning as two half-moons,
and King Bhagiratha born of two vulvas,
who brought down later to its plains, the Ganga.

In the 13th-century Jayadratha's *Haracaritacintamani*,
elephant-headed Malini swallows Parvati's
menstrual blood that flows in the Ganga
to give birth to
our obstacle-vanquisher, Ganesha.

But when science experiments use electric shocks
to impinge apprehension in mice
we see generations
of little mice-grandchildren
growing up with the fear of the smell of
(you guessed it...)
... cherry blossoms.

That's why our frog breathes also through his skin.

Mr. Baker

Mr. Baker sat with a robot
whose eyes went left and right.
The robot knew it all but
not that it was fitted with a new device.

Mr. Baker read books and learnt the violin,
undergoing meditational drills.
He rode the wave, the tiger,
under new yardsticks of rising metrics.
Each year a rainfall.

The robot didn't take sick leave,
it had an intelligent cough, used a deliberate pause.

Mr. Baker had children.
His wife, Sue, worked her fingertips with needles.

She packed their things in stacked boxes
one evening, and over dinner told the girls
the roof of their house had gone off flying
like sails to a wind.

They moved into an aunt's attic.

Copies of Mr. Baker's CV flutter.
Jobs are across the street.
But Mr. Baker fears crossing, looking left and right.

Sue has her fingertips infringed with needles.
Their daughters make space in the attic
from squares to triangles.

The robot is loaded with the next chip.
It can tolerate hunger. Its plastic is tough.

Mr. and Mrs. Baker do not talk much. Their girls are quieter.
He doesn't smile or stand up, Mr. Boss is noticing.
Mr. Baker is lazy, and laziness comes in sizes.
The robot has Profession 3.9 loaded. Its new job is its passion.

Mr. Baker suffers attrition.
Mr. Boss plays a violin –
a quivering pull one way, in the slowest measure
of ungainly high profits.

Mr. Baker's laughter astonishes his family –
watching bills like bird feathers.

He tears his CV. *Let the youth earn – I am 57.*

The robot competes with Mr. Baker's nephew,
before the next chip.

Mr. Baker could never hurt a fly,
but now even a fly can hurt him.

Art Installation

Six walls of a traditional house,
four for patriarchism.

And old men who hate women of confidence,
English speaking – fast and cunning,
who go to the bank, the airport,
making bouquets from spades, sugar from shards,
holding golden bars of golden cages
clanging steel cymbals not utensils

blue & white crockery down the aisles
thunder queens – quietening rooms without words.

When the crockery cupboard empties,
the modern man erects a door
                                        between the floors.

                                                  Conjecture of partition.
                                                  Borders of glacial gasps.

          New crockery fills in.

The old man now seethes over a bitter future
stopping his tongue
                    as the door sways with no latches or bolts

his grandchildren returning to their cacophonous play dough,
under filaments of silence.

As the door hinges
to the wind,

modern men and women
    return to their battles,
        upturning Sisyphean stones
            stacked all around them
                from centuries,
                    brim after
                        brim.

Compatibilities

He's a piggy bank. Put in a coin of kindness
and he stays smiling on the outside,
snug in the corner of a child's room.

I am an attaché of green in a dealer's dirty hands
exchanged and bartered for arson 'n ransom.
In bloodied hands, my value's the same:
whored for the next big thing, the stakes a-changing.

Shouldering dreams over my folded ears—
a ticket of sanctities to major world movements.

But he? Even if taken in kid's delight, he's always placed back
with heartbeats of its owners. Growing sapience in a world
    before adulthood
in a faith of faces, coin-collections.

Yet, friends: I find his corner by the bed's lamp nourishing.
And he, my many-world transits—the cliffhangers I bring.

Beneath the grime, mutual deposit of 25 years—
we are the undersong of assurance.
New experiences, currency-seafarers

both
devalued in time
devalued by the next armed aggression.

Recursive

Under the dome of black, edges of civilizations, stood a soul
as the boatman ferried a little vessel
over mercurial ripples,
melting silvers of moon.

The dark grew, the water strident,
the air dense in perfume.
'How long before we reach? And where are we going?'

The boatman knew he wouldn't see his passenger for long.
Once a soul ended a journey midstream, leaping into the sea.

The boatman didn't want this again,
so he obliged with stories.
'We are heading to a land of a tragic war
between classes.'

He arm-muscled through waves.
'Why?' implored the soul. Its curiosity teetering on
boat-balance – light and quark.

'Because clashes over land, food, women
happen by the powerful.'

'Didn't I come from this place?' said the soul, 'I… remember.'

'You shouldn't. Your past is to be forgotten.'

'But this is my future too now, isn't it?'
'Yes. For now you are to be born a Dalit.'

The soul saw its future. The boat juddered.
Time emerged 'n was born
in the midst of fire
in the land of the running
utensils, helter skelter, strewn possessions,
mud homes burning and bodies.

The baby recognizing the henchmen
of its past life,
as they ravaged,
cursed with the hoards of synapses,
the constructs of his own scheming.

Wasn't this the villager's land that he had wanted?
Its men, its women, its children?
Its treasure boxes and minerals?

Swaddled in a smoked blanket,
he scrunched his face,
like a torn rope from the sky,
opening his mouth
and wept

a tiger's howl and cry.

Overdone

This is the actress
known for her emotiveness:
the quiver of eyebrow,
the flicker of smile;
who grew older
but still wanted younger roles,
younger men.

So she cured her wrinkles, laugh lines
and crow's feet with
heavy neurotoxin.

Now the gleam of her face is total.
But less emotion passes through the cage
of her face.
No grief or sorrow stirs,
love or anticipation.
Neither in real nor on celluloid.
Her feelings grow, rather underskin like water
beneath unyielding tiles,

become the running groundwater
of the river of her life.

Somna

I walk the trail of adolescent shadows
between wakefulness and sleep.
Primitive awakenings of my ancestors –
the Jekyll and Hyde of moon-types.

Drifting into other places like a con artist,
under blankets of theta waves in limbic sensing.
With gene-memory, a vortex of smudging trails
behind curtains of my cortex.

The night closes its lids on partial dangers,
the quivering of arrows, shooting like stars.

I lay awake even in orgasms. There are no latches on my doors.
The doors are in my head, unbolting the light in my nerve,
spotting darkly guns at trigger points.
Like migratory frigate birds
that fly for months in their sleep.
Behind shut eye, alert,
searching the dark stars through the third eye.

The rain in the abyss holds up summers
as secrets give in,
sheltering the unspooling of dress-rehearsals.
Survival of revivals.

A candle worth of hope upsets the trail
at the end of the tunnel,
as the morning moon gloats on sleeping pills,
musky odors of daydreams.

Not even the adultery of vodka works on my gut
in the upstream rivers of denial,
– sips of forgiveness metabolizing,
continuums of realization.
Prolonging the hindrances of surrender
to the shadows that pull
over the longitudes of night.

Loafer

Smoking brainwaves of an unknown city
fish skins on paper
I recall skeletons of caper
amid scuffles on a wooden settee.

Old faces burning to new-earth effigies
framed by fireplaces of surrender,
opinions of world departures,
I resist feel-good ditties.

Hoarding empires, as windchimes quiver
I reimagine an intertwining of extremities.

Some things left for another blight,
some things devoured in slur and slight,
my enmities seeming like amenities
in this cultish café of ol' and *de novo* half-lights.

Piano

To the highest pitch of skylight
on the parapet, he leans ears outstretched
in his friend's apartment.

Away from the soundboards of scuffle,
hammer to strings striking under thumb riffs
as his nails clutch balcony-dirt.

Pitching his heart like an instrument
plucking lesser notes
across his breath and birdcage,
he lunges a harpsichord of coup de grâce,
clavichord of sufferance in octaves.

a scale above the surf and gray sea
deepest breach, highest treble.

He looks at the house. Still, of promising velocity,
hitting resonance – a gut wrench in intervals,
stopping vibrations of release, steadying himself,
perspiring to the wind

as the road glistens from the coast –
sequence of arpeggios.

He watches goosebumps of traffic,
workers digging for new cable,
the lovers at Marine Drive
a forgotten rosary – faraway cemetery.

He and himself – riffs in his head
– crevasses exposing broken contracts
and memory holding black and white keys
of pink-cheeked childhoods

a future under sweating palms,
flashing through firmaments of self
notes, chromatic scales of diffidence,
when he lets go of the ledge.

Solitary

Like light leaves after years,
iterating the static of spheres,
the orangutan exhales warmth
monographing embrace
into winter's foliage,
as time loses scope.

Young as a blank square, nurtured for years
at its mother's teat, beat, emerging from dark art
growing from snugness, luxurious as a shaft,
it goes deep into the forest: light into cave
to live alone
for a thousand years.

No ruffle, or safety of spring meets its spirit
yet as strong as an inflorescent flame
it cinders,
while winter speaks in autumn's
barbed tongue.

Crinkles of Wings

Orange tongues flare a timeless pendulum,
around my unmoving vertebrae.
My body is a country of shadows,
echoing sunset conversations.

Wheels limp, a memory-alternating tungsten,
like spoons 'n chopsticks.
Rivers choke the sea of my syllogism.

In ruptured colors of autumn I sense the
liminal movements of leaves,
rain falling, summers running thin,
the wind in clothes, cloudbursts of Gulmohars,
the march of pariahs, anarchy of crows,
the genocide of sparrows.

The flickering screensaver in ant-rasping dialog.

I know *them* by their names now: *boo boo* and *bobo.*
I have learnt to say *no* when they knock on the door.
Sometimes they come into my daydream,
to blindfold my sedentary and nomadic sides
– quotidian qualia.

Fatigue sculpting my body in painkillers.
The wilderness of days melting ligaments of rage.
Time hewn in new thoughts… so I don't suffer cold feet.

If light is a spectrum, sight too is.
You see of me first
what I see of myself last.

Pain is unseen, if it isn't a wound.
My biggest goal of being accepted.
Talk to me
first.
Don't move or tip over me.

It is music that resounds hope
in chimeras of hollow steel or bone.

Love

Late in the evenings when the forest grew sounds,
the smell of rain on dung, jungle of danger,
he kept arsenal in green –
raw blood and just-alive meat.

A man with a heart – he loved animals.
Off a spinning hunt and new game,
he watched them through his binoculars.

The forest guards, sleeping…

A leopard played with a boy's carcass
through his camera-on-terrain.
He killed it in spite, roasted, and ate it.
No dogs came near him after that.
An unusual smell coming off him.

The forest guards, sleeping…

A forest official once asked for buffalo horn,
sent him to kill bovine.
He killed its baby too,
his head and stomach churning.
Until came a new forest-range officer,
who told him of the role of every
animal in the ecosystem.

He gave up hunting, and began
tranquilizing rogue elephants
for a living.

But when it rained,
the gates of the forest broke.
Villagers turned away by floods
became hunters and poachers again, like him.

They wouldn't have gone to danger
but forest-protection officials grew hungry
for a taste of rare meat
every now and then.

The forest guards, sleeping…

Strings

The only thing Shalom remembered with his last breath,
was his violin stolen at a Berlin concert.

Stradivari's 960 violins – one surviving the ocean-blues
well-photographed.
A Stradivarius located in Chor Bazaar, *shor bazaar*
legend states if you lose anything –
like Queen Victoria sailing to Bombay,
you will... find it there.

Son Solomon makes a trip to Mumbai's middlemen.

But the violin is gone.
A lady has taken off, just minutes ago...
Solomon finds her address. Dhobi Talao.

Mrs. Dias' husband Frederick
played the violin when young,
before his father forced him into the 9–5's.
unburnt talent : *burning bodies*
Frederick bought a plane ticket
to watch Shalom.
It could have been him
thirty-five years ago
when he entered the green room,
downplaying the fiddle to the confines of his jacket.

Hollow wooden body resting between chin and chest
a scar ensconced suture-like across his neck
to the empty cough of lung and rib
with nothing to buy medicines,
Mrs. Dias sells old junk.

The non-artist son of a virtuoso understands this:
core of lost dreams, non-inheritance of genes, disapproved
    childhood
while his sister Greta is the maestro, protégé.

Solomon keeps the violin back in Frederick's chest.
When Greta hears of it, she yells
You don't understand a thing
about an artist's life... While the non-artist
son wonders
        if she understands
                        a thing
                                about life.

Layers of Etiquette

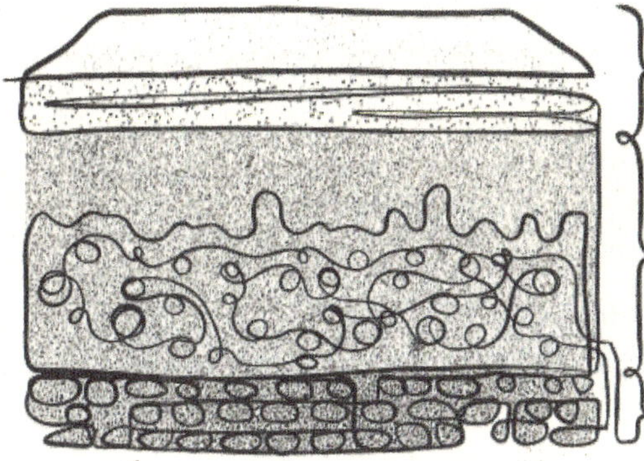

with them in solidarity

we like if they can blend,
assimilate and
not interfere

we don't mind if they
are clean and intelligent
despite being inferior

we hate them

Departure

See how he wilted as soon as she left.
He grew a silver stubble – deserts on skin, as soon as she left.

The water ran out of sinks.
The house grew reed thin, as soon as she left.

The flowers turned twigs, the puppy skeletal,
roaches gained freedom, rats ran amok, as soon as she left.

The country turned alien, borders anti-national.
Clouds and planets lost their names as soon as she left.

Her body oozed virulence from every chasm.
And I, *Saanjh*, seamed her with cotton, fervor, and good
riddance as soon as she left.

street artists' tips

Atonement

The tropical painting on glass is flaking,
after the rioting, the commotion, the stampede,
before the weight of explanations,
in the sheen of UV light, fracking
short- and long-waves polarizing
strains of deceit, fluorescing.

The restorer has walked in – brittle himself,
with a stereo-binocular microscope strapped to his head,
a fiber-optic light
and all the gadgets in place.

Removing old varnish that clouds the view
of a golden bird
flying into the blue,
crammed with golden eggs.

Sensitive glass
changing temperaments of sentiments,
shocks of bright spots.

The restorer heats testaments crystalline – an excess of alkali
composites of conquest, under the N word (*nationalism*),
prefixed with *anti*, from time to time.

He refills, retouches surface level losses,
for a unity of composition.

The picture gains old esthetics
in pigments of resins.
New promises, mantras, Goebbels-tested
with never-aging properties, rectifying conditions
of coloring,
weathering hope with crizzling theories.

Marqueteiro now holds the painting up to air
a tarnish of new varnish – promise in believability
with adhesives of hypothesis,
synthetics of adjectives,
catharsis-stories.

The picture in quadruplicity
is then hung in the left wing,
right wing, central wing,
ceiling
of our ancient heart museums.

To Daraza

Those who do not know history climb the Thar Express,
not its brumal roofs,
as hibernal winds destroy distance,
cloud specters over *chulha* smoke.
From barren trees,
dusk falls beneath the international train,
blood seeping into benumbed fruit.

The engine noise suicides at Zero-Point Station—
final point of immigration—perforated edges of identity,
season tickets of contraband memory.

The air nippy along the ears, long checks of passports. *blue.*
green.
A stinging wait for visa in sunset gale,
freezing through smokes from Bidi No. 30,
smells of *kebab*s, and *paratha*s under warm blankets.

On the other side lies a dragnet of overused British-laid rails,
for trade.

She peels Sachu's verses from a locket
over her frayed neck—
an unused key of a rusted trunk
thrown into a well
of hewn ancestors. Years ago.
She quenches starlight in Sachu's *suras*: *Where crowds are, there*
I am not.

Those who do not know history click images of the sun-rouged galaxy,
blood thawing in skies,
chocolate-biscuit wrappings fleeing to artic metal floors
of a carriage of new border-crossings
in old silences of one million basal sighs
disemboguing . . . ten million permanent scars.

She now translates the Sufi's verses.
Our bond was created for a reason. Slumber has created illusions.
Endless ones from endless books. Moving to fervid cores.
Smuggled agony in an Amritsari museum for refugee things.

Sindh did not remain, a Sindh mail connecting . . .
At Munabao, the TTE pokes bags, inspecting vegetables in a hotcase,
pulling down beddings, opening suitcases.
Everything is a weapon: a one-year-old child,
a cone of boiled groundnuts,
almonds from a tin, skittering . . .

The road to Sachu is fraught in old Gurmukhi,
words slipping over postmodern tongue.
I was sitting by the roadside, when the path became clear.
No one wants its cipher to enter Mehran's alluvial plains,
the Indus River, the Thar Desert, the Kirthar Mountains.
Sachu himself was in search of peace. For long.
To forgive the hangover from an inflamed life.

Freezing joints, the train trundles cries, wired borders, mass
troops, customs officers.
She will go to Karachi, Hyderabad in Sindh, Quetta
in this train for the poor, where everyone carries temperate
gifts:
coconuts, *elaichi*s, pressure cookers, paan, cashew.

Many don't fill forms or know to signature.
They rely on one family member's passport for all.
A married daughter who misses chow mein from Hyderabad,
India.
A childless Bhilwara millworker travelling to see his nieces.
A Kashmiri shawl merchant visiting his father's grave.
An Indore jeweler's parents living on both sides.
A Bollywood hopeful who loves India, more than her parents.
A Nalanda tailor adopted by an Indian uncle for a better life.
A clerk from Palanpur . . .
A peanut seller questioned about the limits of
the South Asian Free Trade Agreement.

As the train stalls, time in limbo, she translates Sachu—
If I interpret love for all times, a hundred resurrections will pass,
and yet my commentary will not end.
She waits for momentum now, in any direction:
the savoir faire of time,
the explicit march of reminiscence,
or just plain exaltation: a levitation.

My friend is translating Sufi poet Sachal Sarmast's verses. After an evening of speaking to her about her translation-journey, this poem emerged. Sachal Sarmast was born in Daraza. It is said he never left Daraza.

Cellular P.O.W.

Minutes, frozen. Hours irrelevant. Shaped in impulse, racing
pulses. Never thinking of the never-ending.
Metal. Mesh. Electrical fence. Reform or retribution. A
moment that changes. Everything.
Until laws change, rebalancing breath.
Concrete bed and table beneath city, within a sewer, quarry,
dungeon, squalid condition.

Gallery of slavery.

But no capital punishment, mutilation, flagellation.
Dog. Sensor. Gate. Tower. Place of chains. Iron manacles.
Hierarchy of ruffians. Offenders, vagrants, felons, debtors,
cannibals.

Our movement is lethal.
Legal in a new season.
A nation gaining independence.

A diet of silence. Learning restraint. No talks of riots or
escapes. Breaking stone, soul, bone. Building roads, forts,
mines. Work camps. Houses of correction.
Meeting thyself, under duress, prison dress, years of sentence,
food meals, friendship.
Pinched, punched, branded armory of memory, hood of
meditation. No mirrors on the wall.
Shadows bending. Conscience taking another route.
Invisibles remolding – ideas of home, bone, food, chair,
backrest, spine, tea, time with family, babies.
Trapped beneath a vacation of muteness.
Myth of music. Countdown in the head. Words in bibles. Texts
that sing. Think.

For every reason.

Gall. Gullet. Guillotine. Seagull.

Keep information vacant. Eyes of a sinking ship. Don't get into fights. Stay amicable.

A morgue of flesh, corroded edges, limp limbs, dead toes, high intention: hunger, despise, no pretense.

Everybody is the same. It's all in the mind, all in the mind.

Take a holiday. Island of memory.

Mind in clouds. Circles of regret. Flesh in wrinkles, scars purple.

Meeting thyself in solitude.
Iron grindings, internalizing
the largest filing system of civilization.

Archiving.
Arrival.

War Specials

As we went to war over animals on our plates,
pigeons too were seized by their wing-flaps, rings around claws;
a phone number and address with *Shakargarh* and *Narowal* in
Urdu.
Spy pigeons, un-believing of borders, photographed, carried
messages, guided bombs,
like knight's warhorses that bit and kicked,
and elephants that were machines.

As we went to war over animals on our plates,
animals were politicized too: pigs squealed, camels patrolled,
mules carried supplies, oxen – artillery,
moose were trained not to be gun-shy for deep-snow cavalry,
and dogs threw their weight or sniffed out mines.
Monkeys dipped in oil 'n fire, were thrown into enemy territory.

When the seagulls flew they carried torpedoes,
dead rats, explosives in their bellies.
Vultures, pelicans thrown to air came back darkly and powderly.

The new recruits were sharks with brain implants.
Cats controlling vermin. Chickens detecting poison.
Bones and beaks in war memorials.
It wasn't only Noah's dove that returned after the flood.

Molotov cocktails.

We haven't otherwise even left the bacteria, virus, fungi…

Embedded with heavy explosives –
unseen beasts, second only to racial slurs,
we now have *w.o.r.d.s.* to reproduce in our bodies and ears

time over time, over our grand internet,
staying in memory,
trolled by embittered species.

And words?
They have a separate gallantry.

Capsule

Our conversations end mid-sentence.
Our stories hang on bones.
The split-second splitting of eardrums.
Tube-lights, iron rods, switchboards.

My spine is a high-voltage shock.
All pawns standing have fallen down, crisscrossed.
Some burnt, some charred.
Someone's hand is on my shoulder,
a stomach cushions my head.
The exhaust fan is on my chest,
a disembodied finger carries a briefcase yet.

A shoe has left its feet – the puce of near-death.

Mumbai '06, 11th July, 6.53 p.m.
reeks in chorus of smoke,
air riffs in rose quartz.
As the evening sun-wheels,
death comes in pressure cookers,
copper wires dangling.

Wreck, wretch, wreathing
– entrails of deadening silence
in fire, nickel, gunmetal.
Dissected battleship of RDX, ammonium nitrate.
The ruptures of a cinerous breathing.

Italy, Lima, Madrid, London,
Moscow, Istanbul, or Brussels.
I could have been anywhere
in gainsboro and platinum.

When I stumble upon the train station,
ghosts walk up to me.
I can see their screams and sirens.

My heart is a bomb.
And we wait for it to explode.

Place

Emancipation is white,
gray skin dotted in shark bites.

Cut to the tail – damages from a fishing line,
braided in helplessness, fissured visions –
pneumonia and an eye ulcer,

they found him on a beach
and named him Sulphur.
Seven months, they nursed him in rehab.
When he could hunt fish they tied a radio collar
and sent him into the causeway.

He was stiff at first. *What is home?*
If not in the direction of an aquarium.

Home is how warm it gets between the flaps –
liquid charcoal around the shadows and bends.

Chiaroscuro of red light and a dorsal fin spattered,
attacked by a tiger shark.
Rescued too late. A tennis-ball of a heart,
'n smoke in the irises.

White skin in a brown country
300 years of *hukumat* –
throbbing natural organs
and still 'a bloody primitive'

Porcelain assumptions
through imperial glints. *Where is home?*
If not in the direction of a museum.

Medium-sized decorative installation.
Hung in a hallway on a nail.
Stuffed with rags,
synthetic ideologies
speaking shark-syllables.

Sulphur is a life-like specimen –
knifed with a wider smile over his face.
'Sometimes we can't stop nature in its coursing.'

Brown skin in a white country
100 years of citizenship –
embalmed, upholstered
and still 'a bloody immigrant'.

Conjoined

They came – joined at the abdomen
sharing intestine, lung, a urinary passage,
one anus: faith and fundamentalism.

Devotion over materiality, literal in visceral
addicted to their mother's milk
'n her approval.

Paranoid about toys, keeping grace,
unburdened in the loci of controlling bladders,
measuring deeds, vows of creation,
giving back in wholes.

Advertised as Goddess
two heads, eight limbs

refusing to get to each other's side
when either of them was kissed.

They had emergency operations
to separate from slim viscera,

but it has taken a thousand years
and still counting…

City 101

Built with bones and grass over the fringe of songs,
the lake rippling in lyric,
this new city doesn't have dust for a thumbprint.
No wet cement freezes footmarks.
No letters in boxes. No letter boxes.
Telepathic telephone lines.
No shoes, no tyres. No tarmac or asphalt.
Urban sprawl. Urban mall. Workspaces across the street in
walking lines.
Graffiti out in the twilight. Food, gambling, nightlife,
and home corners for strays in 200 drainage miles
for city floods.
The waste under skin of soil. Even the grass is edible.
Plates made of dried leaf.

But when we dug beneath this, we found another city
100 feet below with rustic cobblestone in its stomach
a subterranean of 35 acres. 60 miles of roads,
a television studio, murals, cafeteria, pub –
in case of a nuclear attack.

And further below we found another city –
33 miles of catacombs against medical clinics, schools,
theaters, and a roller rink.
Food from mushroom farming
in case of a nuclear attack.

And under this, another
200 miles of caves hollowed from limestone
for corpse disposal, quarry walls,
a postal service, data center, cheese-aging facility,
mushroom farms, caved out of bluffs
of a giant mine, hideouts during an old war
above a river.

There are only seven stories in the world:
man against man, woman, nature, against himself,
against God, society, or caught in the middle,
This has to be one of them then.

Thoughts recurring in patterns, performing history.

These cities threatening to cave in
from all that's above
much before a nuclear attack.

Battered House

Defending freedom in its hour of danger, Martin Luther King's opaque-headed shooter got 99 years in prison.

In the year Kennedy was killed, Vostok 6 returned with
Valentina Tereshkova – the first woman in space.
The year Gandhi was murdered, an entire population of
Checheno-Ingushetia had been deported, killed in Siberia's
harsh weather.
A decade after Martin Luther King's death, the genocide of
Acholi and Lango people under Idi Amin had concluded.
In 1971, lakhs of Bengali Hindus in Bangladesh were
terminated.
And the year after Indira Gandhi was assassinated, hundreds of
Sikhs were massacred.

Rajiv Gandhi was bombed with a basket of flowers by
women Tamil Tigers, and Malcom X shot by the Nation
of Islam.

Lincoln was called out to twice before the last bullets, and
Caesar stabbed 23 times
for the Roman empire to emerge from the republic.

When the majority is strong, it has guns...
When the majority is the minority, it has pleas...

Sometimes many killed one. Sometimes one killed many.
The sway, the sway for land, for territory.

Dried bones of contentions over slit wrists of
cartography.
From whose womb did you come?
What be the color of your skin?
Dialect of tongue? How you pray, love, and fuck?
What is on your plate? Who is on your bed?
What is the color of your
blood?

Fathers and mothers (of nations) massacred in mystery,
Aung San, planned by confidantes, colleagues, security
guards, fans,
where children died in genocides of
Holocaust, Holodomor,
Cambodian, Armenian,
Rwandan, Greek,
Assyrian, Zunghar,
Porajmos, Bangladesh,
Burundian, Kurdish,
Guatemalan, Herero and Namaqua,
Bosnian, Selk'nam, and Yazidis.

Akin to nature's avalanche and sinkholes,
blizzards, heat storms, limnic eruptions,
droughts, famines, cyclonic storms,
sun flares and wild fires,

with the earth's temperatures rising,
the house pillows in fleece, all the glass shattered, the
shards strewn.

And the first time we heard of *wasted children* –beneath their weight and height, 6.3 million dying under the age of five: 17,000 each day,

while another assassination, another genocide is plotted.

The house pillows in ruins, all the glass shattered, the shards and fleece strewn.

Ground Up

Once the haze lifted, the hot war had ended.
Empires were lost and imperial powers thwarted.

Many fled, or were removed forcibly
in the face of armies. Nationalist movements begun,
and forgetting was as important
as the how-to of remembering.

Schools didn't teach history,
and textbooks were blank.

After the mist lifted, trojan horses
of marxism and socialism galloped
over the murky earth of capitalism.

Some still believed they had fought
on higher moral grounds.

After the blur lifted,
the dead were piles of rubble.
Year zero had begun.

Bridges, forests, vineyards were brume
and a diet of 1000 calories were tulip bulbs.

Babies were orphaned and women aborted
a million spoils of their wombs.

After the veil lifted, on wobbly legs
came the cavalrymen of cataclysm

– famine and pestilence,
but also microwaves, atomic weapons,
power and penicillin.

After the mizzle lifted, the cold war had begun.

Death reappeared to see how nations rose
from their torn knees, wrecked ankles
over a foxtrot of shards, catalogue of ashes,
countries that had broken their tongues and ridges.

And their people who admitted that they were not
the only victims.
They too had raped and killed, drawn up the blood.

Now textbooks have disturbed memories,
not white and dark histories.

The generations after
bent low over their work
—had ten times at hand.

They did not look up for years,
at the beauty of the early slate skies
or the late stone skies.

But kept moving:
to stir, to sing, to rue, to sob,
to stand, to cross.

So to transition…
to turn a page of history…

Mask

He wore one when he was born
of driftwood, feathers, skin-bone
distorting features: round eyes,

nose as long as a fence
narrow chin.

He told us he was God. Master carver
down generations of puppetry, mime, farce
with harlequins, hobby horses, bluff
movable jaw in a ritual dance
at marriage or circumcisions.

But go hunting.

A man was dropped into the Atlantic,
graves are still breathing.
Bodies are containers of mutilation.
The ethnographic question
always:
violent and visceral.

Your brothers' breath looms in our rooms
cold bodies on riverbeds.

Disguise
        to preside over the carnival of cannibals:
vestige, vessel, visage.

Go up in smoke. Communicate with the forest spirits.
Grow a monstrous head to ward off evil.

Seek a way to the spiritual.
Talk not of sports or religion.
Rely on food, weather, fable.

Cover gashes across faces.
Learn the philosophy of the shard
with protective armors, burn masks, taciturnity
in wars.

Turn to shamans, angels, ancestors,
when the cartograph convulses.
Contract rape – an interim measure
in the hardening of smothers.

Let wisdom seek through war paint.

The breath you left is in our prayers.

Bodies are weapons of healing
too.

Talk in eloquence, hide winters of darkness.
Encipher language, give beauty to bruise.

Break into song. Bread.
Wounds bleed, scars fade, bones mend.
Optimism wins at the end.

Now when he is dead, his funeral mask is of
gilt, copper, lead –
good-luck talisman.

But who's the enemy? Who the ally? Jonah in a whale's belly.

Everyone is equal behind the mask.

The story remains the same.

Investigation: A Report

Long before the bomb blasts at Plaza Cinema,
Zaveri Bazaar, Century Bazaar,
parking lot in Katha Bazaar, Sahar airport,
Air India Building, Sea Rock hotel, Bombay Stock Exchange,

the thing called *kala sabun*
like what my missus uses
to wash our dirty utensils
was found.

We saw... what we saw only in the movies
grenades, rifles, magazines, pistols,
by men on our coast
opening cartons without a smile

when cars, jeeps, trucks
were stopped at the toll –
by customs officers
with false alerts.

After the noise shattered
our eardrums
the police found Dr. Sapatnekar
and his deep sea divers
ebbing into 25 feet of sludge
to find brown cakes
at the bed of the Nagla creek.

They picked a broom maker,
porters, loaders, boatmen (like me)
who loaded sacks of iodex into jalopies
for minimum wages.

And two kilometers off Srivardhan
in a lake, they found floating
rocket-like objects, projectiles,
pipe bombs 'n ammunition.

The men from nearby houses were
stripped, burnt with smoldering cig butts,
beaten up at the police station

until those turned out to be
spindles of a textile mill,
overturned by a truck,
ignored by village people.

How none of us could say RDX.
Nor see the *hindola*s of revenge
for the December 1992, January 1993 riots
were an answer to innocent Muslims being killed

to avenge innocent Hindus being killed
to avenge innocent Muslims being killed
to answer innocent Indians being killed
to avenge innocent humans being killed
in many many Indias…

---

hindola – merry-go-round

Resurrection

In all his 40 years, Jesus wouldn't have guessed
an early death, a career with the surround sound of miracles
He wouldn't have expected his wafer-body
to be taken so seriously –
Crusades in the Mediterranean against the jihadis.

On the oriental side, Buddhism ripening under a Gaya tree,
Spanish inquisitors, Portuguese conversions in Goa
Catholicism fructifying from American baptists
and the British trade colonies
North-East India speaking Christianity.

The most interesting years of his life
missing from history
And then wars for peace, reconversions,
pro-life and pro-choice conflicts.

Kings on cards, and humpty dumpty –

a dream in someone's heart
of breaking down churches
to avenge a destruction of 300 temples, 300 years ago…

Religion becoming recursive
One denomination, after demolition
a scamper of time, traffic, technology.

That when the Houses of spirituality severed,
releasing sighs from altars, *garbha-grihas*,
dar-e-mehrs, *takhalmmlolts*, and *kaabahs*
devotees were trapped in unbroken repentance.

No prayers heard. No faith returned.

The gods who had no business in modern thesis,
mythology films, or wall calendars
left –
their dynasties, misappropriated…

Christ, Zoroaster, Allah, Nanak, Ram
now pilgrimize the bazaar and boulevard.

Partisan's Village

Break down a temple, church. Build a mosque.
Break down a mosque, temple. Build a church.
Break down a church, mosque. Build a temple.
But where's god in these building blocks of civilization?

In the splendid dog fights of the bigots
the reinterpretations of religion… or history

if we thought feminism battled through new skins
of leninism, marxism, communism,
capitalism, socialism, dictatorship, and democracy,
we did not see that ideologies governed
from one mind,
crossed over 100 years
to candle marches, *andolan*s, revolutions
blooming into political parties.

Power-brokering disunities, new diversities,
selective idioms
heart *versus* mind *versus* hands *versus* feet
tongue *versus* tongue *versus* tongue.

The eternal love for aggression.
Shouting down voices
drowning rivers diverted,
quenching villages,
parching others.

Within four pillars of slavery. savagery. lethargy. whataboutery.
the third eye force-ripening
through the bureau of unemployment.

It is then that they planted 10,000 saplings
uprooting 10,000 trees
for a city's new metro line.

Jallianwala Bagh Mystic

In the community hall of genocidal refugees, everyone has
collective memory. When you are dead the reasons for your
death become gibberish.
The singer of Auschwitz tells of the barracks he last met his
beloved in, before gas chamber. The Rwandan of the hacking
at his neck and how thoughts on the universe spilled faster than
blood. The Mirchpur Dalit of fear and fire roasting his
70-year-old Haryanvi body.
An Afghan of measuring against a lynchpin; still holding
his head like a chalice. A Native American withholding her
disparate body and Spanish fetus. The 6-year-old girl from
Sandy Hook possessive of her pink ribbon. The Haitian Creole
practicing his 'r' in parsley (*pereji*) to avoid ethnic devastation.
One of the mentally ill from the T4 1941 program.
We all sit at this table.
Joined by the Jallianwala Bagh mystic's tune of:
why the earth is always russet.
The Jallianwala Bagh mystic died in a well with 120 frenzied
others. Death by wishful drowning. Sweet Amritsari waters
filling his nostrils, sockets, lungs, stomach, gut.
No one disowns death. No one disavows treachery.
You recognize propaganda as real. Fake narratives, gospel.
That General Dyer could have teleported, 100 years ago, on 13
April 1919
son of an Irish farmer, shepherd on a diet of hunting, snipe-
shooting
found weird sheep flocked together, and fired
from a machine gun fitted on an armored vehicle.

Until Udham Singh pulled two bullets down O'Dwyer's brain
21 years later.
All sheep going to the pastures of redemption.

The Jallianwala Bagh mystic plays his one-stringed *tumbi* – a
thrum linking last whimpers in peaks and troughs of harmony,
It is not over ... he croons, *blood from the ink pot of antiquity,*
to spill for the quill of history.
There we see coming on one leg a Rohingya Muslim.
His smile as a torn blanket on a cold winter's morning.

Parliaments of variety

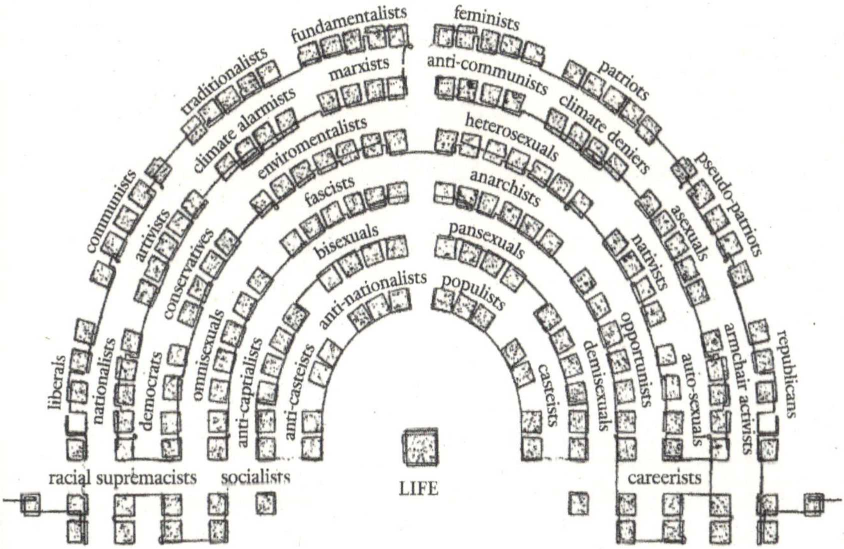

Hexagonal

Once an invisible city of unseen borders
grew around an invisible tower, fenced by invisible walls
of men and women in seasonal cycles of clashing worldviews
in homage to Mandeville's bumbling city.

Where when virtues turned bad for business, the vices rang
true
as they traded prejudice in the black markets of gray pieces
of the new chessboard,
in the heresy of intolerant spews
near hamlets of treachery, boulevards of love
in suffrage to Mandeville's stumbling city.

Coffin makers, bomb-and-gun makers
sweetshops, sweatshops, arms and ammunition dealers,
all turned disillusioned –
doctors and drill-makers and House-of-God hope-makers
in the footloose swirl over Dante's Inferno
chained to their psychiatric couches and chairs
near ghettos of prudence, prefectures of limbo
in assemblage to Mandeville's fumbling city.

Once when an Elder-hunter threw a bone
into these groomed lawns, the two civilization dogs
killed each other
instead of measuring saw...
learning the art of equality, against the cartilage
near flea markets of justice, crossroads of faith –
falling down Abraham Maslow's pecking order
in patronage to Mandeville's crumbling city.

Each dog should have its own bone
said the Apex of Justice Primate,
and joined in echoes
were the Departments of Wrath, Ministries of Violence
Precincts of Lust, Stadiums of Gluttony,
Blind Alleys of Wisdom, Ringsides of Fortitude
near the gambling dens of virtues, suburbs of sacrilege
in pilgrimage to Mandeville's humbling city.

coins in rivers

Confluence

Waters when they evaporate, meet...
at a global conference, to speak of fish dropouts,
obscura of clouds, near-deaths, hydrological dynamics,
monocultures, and metals:
nickel, lead, chromium, at their beds.

The bend is notional: water for coffee, cane,
banana, paddy,
mills, distilleries,
fertilizer plants.

The Aral Sea was water for cotton
in Uzbekistan:
one shirt drinking 2000 liters,
now more saline than the Dead Sea –
palm-sized, a fossil-tiger's footprint,

plains of salt, toxic dust storms,
fishing towns, now ship-graveyards,
people, sick; dumps of pathogenic weapons
making the summers hotter, winters colder,
the Aral Sea is the Aralkum Desert.

And if seas made maps,
rivers, homes
men, borders.

The Cauvery too is uprising
 – one of the longest-running rivers
over her water share to ripple greens
for Karnataka and Tamil Nadu,
when her sand beds expand for mining
flowing from Brahmagiri
on her way to the Bay of Bengal,
she worries if those warring over her understand

that a river is a person,

like Whanganui of New Zealand
– ancestor of 160 years
that got legal status
through the longest-running litigation
by the Māori people

because mountains too
are equal to men.

The Earth Remembers

The earth remembers
her orange-spotted filefish and quivering trees,
kidnapped polar bears, cods, penguins,
missing corals and golden toads.

Rub-marks against barks
in the smell of territorial piss,
muscle memory of travesties.

She remembers the brink of brink.
Who used what and how much?
Erasing carbon calligraphies – green to gray
temperatures rising in a room
each year
by 2 degrees.

In gatherings of ground-up hurricanes,
prayer songs of beating hearts.
The earth remembers her Chipko movement:
20th century, Rajasthan – Amrita Devi and 363 others
sticking their backs to save the unfelled.

Balding forests in fodder and firewood,
cars making the roads small.
Hands into cave mouths, and tigers
prowling the city banks,
eating up children.

Expropriation in green to rust,
no clocks ticking backward.
The earth remembers the heart of a drying lake,
gut
where all breathe an equal air of light-bulb-promises.

No crisis on the plate, the cost of a dreamer's laissez-faire,
without heat waves, rising sea levels.
Closest to the frontlines with your chest bare
no central heating or cooling systems.
Disproportionate hot and cold places
in lost battles.

The earth remembers her stare.

Housekeeping what gets dirty.
Cleaning up after the dance.
Civil disobedience for unseen ribs.
In the hens and eggs, the cow and her milk,
the land and her mines, green belts 'n deserts.

The earth remembers, her bowels of toxic dump.
Waters polluted, bodies submerged, emissions in worrisome
bubbles.

How much it took to grow a toddler nation against an adult one?
Clean combustion, equalizing a platter,
vacant lots of gardens. *Rust to green.*

Radiations in the face of imperialism, over-consumption,
capitalism, greed.

The earth remembers her severed temper.

Displaced

The fish fly in the night to become stars.
Trees hopscotch;
they knew when they dried – leaves wrinkling, foliage
    thinning.
They gathered honey when the earth got angry
with wild wind knots in their women's hair.
It was time for the rain to let down her tongue,
that she always kept in reserve.

They knew their forests by tigers, leopards, macaques, langurs,
hornbills, and cane turtles.
Their river was a lifeline on their palms.

They didn't know how metal dragonflies could descend from
    the sky.
The sky – as empty as a grieving mother's chest.
    And men came on cycles in shirts and trousers,
    that everyone fled from.

    They would build a dam here, pour concrete into waters.
    Some days the sea ran into the old sweet river,
    spiraling green noxious that grew beside her.

They had to leave their cows.
They had new roots now,
under another *mahua* tree.

They got looms, but no roofs, and no thread.
When the rain broke her lip
their money evaporated like sweat.

Their poultry died of sickness.
Each road was an island
turning bare the walls of school, center, shop.

Some went into the mouths of the forest.
Some lay as still as mud.
Some left for city shanties.
And some like Kalu sat outside their homes

rowing a boat gently
over the new river
stopping right at its center.

There were no fish there,
where many, many feet below
his village, home, and fields still lay.

He talks of the past... haltingly.

The Toys of Chitrakoot

From *bhurkul* to *gular*, mango, *shisham*, green bamboo,
slow-heated, drawing moisture off limbs
bodies passed through lime glue, bound with tamarind seed paste,
the toymaker traces features,
fine-stroking with hammer, filing paint, bringing dolls to life
under wigs.
He remembers his children, vacant-chested, sent back from school,
            kitchen stoves clutching cooking pots with no food
                        – leaves of cacti
lacquering on lathe
colored by his expectant wife with *alta* and turmeric.
A brush from goat's hair, clay, oil, lac, dye spread amid dreams
– rags, watercolour, red sanders carving kingly elephants,
                annihilating trains to build bridges,
                    bridges for aeroplanes, rattles,
                horse carriages, to make new women.
As the rain chisels flatland, plastic bubbles from machines
      – Chinese toys overcasting the market
                given to
                    sacrificing a child's play of
              pots, teacups, dirt, rope, cardboard boxes,
        before the gods on eves of weddings, rites of passages
                in chorus-fingers of *samsaric* sawdust.
Now concave-eyed, sculpting,
the toymaker makes a toy for himself
for when his children leave to become
mechanical engineers in irreverent cities.

Trapped in a crucible of water,
rippling reflections from *dudhi sundari, punki, koraiya* wood
in warehouses of idols
with no boon powers –
bangle-stands that act like fortresses.
His minuscule house dangles with hay
to the winds.

The toymaker plants molten gobs around a pipe
and blows from the reverberating caves of his ribs,
splintering breath, burying his howls deep,
blossoming glass moons under cloud-capitalisms,
as the rain dwindles all his footprints
on the rough earths of Chitrakoot.

The Secret Life of a Roll

In rectangular wilts of *tendu* leaves
crushed in gold powder, *tambakoo* appeased,
rolled by fingers of women and
children of chalk-dust fallacies.

Big Brother watching with hundred eyes
of a 40-crore industry
not all of them shut all the time,
baking in a furnace without a helmet.
One end of a thread tied,
tapping potent dust –
pension schemes of respiratory ailments.
Where does all the smoke go? All the tendrils?

Rejected beedis into the maker's lap.
Sold, unbranded on the streets.
Gutka and low wages
competing in the market of
unregistered workmanship.

Smoldering at the other end
heavy levels of nicotine
fires stolen by Prometheus
in a reed from Olympus and the sleeping Zeus.

Heavens to earth,
inhaling light and keeping shut.

A professor of health
denies toxicity,
trivializing secondhand smoke –
independent scientist – stooge of green lust,
connects it to lifestyle and the entertainment industry.

When the cameras are on
the whistle-blowers are always judged: *mentally unstable.*

That's what happens to radiance
or fire-givers chained to cliffs,

a wrathful vulture eating livers
growing mutating cells
for a cancer-from-tobacco
500-crore industry.

Strange Cities

Strange cities
remind us of a village with its doors open, resisting a bridge
noon siestas with no iron locks
a sea with fish but no postal code or hospital,

of a city on a rig in the Caspian Sea – 120 kms of road,

a town at the base of a volcano, where people lived with gas masks

or a ship-city that never left canal, with football fields

even dwarfs living in pink tutus with a miniature police force,
political system, fire brigade.

The walled city in Kowloon uprooting from anarchy
not imploding on itself and

another city built on scrapes and salvage, with a
clock tower of garbage.

A town built around a conspiracy of a
devil's statue at the gates holding holy water.

Make what you want to make of these,
as tourists flock like keep-savers,

A town in Brazil for only women,
started by a banished adulteress; now encircled by rainforest,

its epicene dwellers not kissing a man
in years.

These strange kibbutz allowed flakes to flutter,
crossroads to move like sun dials, wheels to jive time
over bubble-wrappings of disharmonies,
chrysanthemum blurs of blueprints

like another city: Auroville
that doesn't exchange money and has no sets of rules

with factories for cloud-making

giving us the notion
that strange people in strange cities
is a very normal thing.

Food Bowl

Where else, if not this land scattering seeds to wind,
waiting for the shaft of ripe sky harvesting crops of rain?
Take from the sky if it gives
the ground in falling water levels, bullock over till,
credit from middlemen, seeds, ads for pesticides, poor irrigation,
arsenic and mercury – a cancer train from Bhatinda to Bikaner.

Alcohol on empty stomachs.
Take babies with no brains, the resistance of pests, and
friendly insects dying.
Take cotton disembarking in clouds in crucifix branches,
hills like salt pans in the ritual of GDP,
no gunk on biodiversity: soil or species.
Take the backstory of a tiffin,
law into your hands, a sip from the tin.

Under colonial-keeping these were just *injuries*.
Take the widow, her debt 'n inheritance.
No marriage for her – indentured servant.
Take late rain from a ditch at a point
the baton changes hands off the green revolution…

Take hundred spoons from a bowl, in the highest-stressed
  profession.
Our land exporting cereals, with images of India Gate, Taj Mahal,
and a woman's round face like a plate. *Annapurna devi*
four hands to give grain, hold vessels, ladles.

Take her god husband – like the government – telling her
life is an illusion,
Take her anger, churn of earth to barren.
Hunger waking in bodies
even the Buddha needing a meal before illumination.

Take a toss of the last coin,
in the gamble of the huge gap
the fact that *Annapurna devi*
has still not returned.

New World Order

These forms that carry knowledge
in algebraic shapes
of mythological immortality

were brought to earth for teaching time
in syllabus –
to kill, heal, harm,
sow, and reap.

Now visions disappear, rousing the wrong answers
with the wrong questions.
Chug-a-lugging the weight of shallowness.
Milestones of a spiritual compass.

No diet of lion or swine,
bone marrows of bears.
No bowing or kissing of hands or feet,
or succumb.

There was a time, apt listeners cut their thumbs
or let wasps suck thigh-blood for their guru, *gyan*.

Now they open fire, holding their chins, resounding slaps,
rising in stature like seeds that don't sprout
– in gross incubation of rigor.

Visible marks left over their teacher's mouths.
Hyperventilating with the law.

Tempers like smoke rising off factories of disobedience,
addicts, delinquents, chain-smokers,
bringing down the juvenile moon,
tearing hyperreal posters to emerge
premature – victors of revenge.

The fear where pupils reignited
to twice their size with wisdom
is now a destructive path
with a danger of smallness.

Confined to a washroom they ask their gurus for sexual favors.
Caught between worlds in a crevasse of darkness.

No *forever* is marked for them
by their elders
as constellations in night skies.

9 Times Infinity

After Kalinga and the blood of 100,000s when Asoka turned
a new season, he looked skywards and entrusted 9 men with
books, sending them into oblivion.
                                        To make light.
The most powerful subjects: time travel, microbiology,
propaganda, psychological warfare, secrets of anti-gravity,
a language binding spirituality, how to kill a person with
touch, the transmutation of metals, communication with the
extraterrestrial,
secrets of gravitation and instructions on making a *vimana*,
cosmogony and matters of the universe,
speed and its weaponry.
The quivers of a new language – thoughts transferred through
vibe, body language, stares,
and rules for the evolution of societies – the means of
foretelling decline.

The identities of these men remained unknown like the
Rosicrucians, the Freemasons, ancient Egyptians, Tibetan
monks.

if knowledge is power
who might they have become
scoundrels or sages?

carrying poison on the tip of their tongues
without swallowing.

Is knowledge myth? And the World?
If this happened in 273 BC, where is its trickledown effect?

Is a major chase unravelling in the dark
between good societies and bad cults?

Are we to await the elixir into our mouths to stain our lips.
Or do we know it
through new cells in our bodies
a DNA-mutation of epiphanies,

adapting one more degree
to the churning of the axes,
the heating up of environments?

Would we come through or stay half-baked?

banknotes

Chaise Lounge

When the earth spins backwards, it displaces deserts, green lands and rainforests over its face – volte-facing the imaginary axis, twilight zone.
When her head spins backwards… she shadowboxes boredom with the mixing of drinks, as her eyeshadows smudge. No TGIFs for her. Or crumbling igloos in cold.
Reflections in club-toilet cisterns and cesspool gurgles. Raging against a capitalistic world in a retro song-beat from the renegade flower children (of the 1970s).
Theme party – hippie. Gypsy. Out of this world. Destiny's children. Children of god.

When the world capitalizes the day, she lets the night run loose. Mad dog.
Her 30s no different from her 17s – slow strobe of wandering streetlights, wolfing down tequila.

millennium silhouettes –
butts smoldering
on potholed galaxies

Feeling the catharsis of a life never lived, epiphanies never examined. Prolonging time, jutting out her tongue, addicted to selfies, she grows sleep like bonsai and cacti into her body.

When the earth spins backward, it alters wind and oceanic currents.
When her head spins backward, she changes from her tight dress to a bloated one for hangovers.

Crazy outsiders morning-jog, or jaunt to school, work, college as she remembers nameless boys, looking at the bloom of blue moon, fire raging through her belly. Watching the telly for stale news chomping on celery, speaking to her family with a slur – a headache that craves a sip of pungency.
The freedom from mist, fire, ice, and never-ending adolescence.

frozen stars –
half a glass of
migraine

Pav

Eh Pavwali! When I was heckled or eve-teased it was slang for a Goan Catholic girl – *pav* meaning bread. We were supposed to be bread makers, bakers, though no one in our house kneaded dough, maybe roti with the smell of curry on Sunday mornings.
I remember my parents sourcing pav from the pavwala instead, who clinked his bell every evening at our building gates.
It was my job to stop playing and fetch the bread wrapped in newspaper. As I quickly raced up the floors, I would dig my dirty fingers into soft bellies and grab cloudfuls – sweet eucharist melting on my tongue.
I fluffed the crusts in a way that it looked full, delivering their emptiness to my mother's dining table.

bestselling award –
no one congratulates
my best friend

child raped –
trolls discuss
her faith

Conch

Once oysters are nowhere to be found, he searches for *shunks*. 130 Indian rupees an hour for diving. He spends hours, over years, under the glittering blue of coral. The last two minutes of holding his bubbles – as time expands – he follows the path of mollusks.
Digging the seabed to the echoes trapped in the chambers of conch shells. Last gasps of lovers, or the singles that drowned from waterfall-selfies. The suicides holding the murmur of marine life. The ocean… their last simpers.
Drawing out bodies, their hands intertwined, he earns extra notes from the government. Their mouths always in surprise, eyes desolate like empty oysters, water snapshotting their stark breath.
Water graves that unite the logic of logging off, in a soundless lap of a new language. The diver himself going deaf from staying too long underwater, hearing all those secrets.

the echo of fjords –
in the bedroom of marriages
white bangles

Clink

My only lockdown obsession was not outward- or inward-
looking
but of plates and forks, spoons and ladles, long-stem giraffe-
necked wine glasses.
People didn't have food to eat, some went to one meal
rallies took place, poets went to jail...
But as I looked at my navel, the world turned into a small orbit.
In this second wave, I had no oil, no gas, no fuel for sprite,
sunshine, optimism.
All *that* was used up in the first year.
What I had, grew from cutlery~crockery solace
footprints from travels to: Egypt, Seoul, London, Dubai, New
York, Hong Kong, Turkey.
The orange river silt of Chiplun; kiln-baked cups of Murbad,
steel teabags from Britain; blue-and-white Victorian
the square saucers of Korea; gilt-edged cups for kava
the wooden Keralan ladles; the *kotti* spoons of Goa.
I lived to wash and rinse these, offloading them from cupboards
kept otherwise for a rainy day or special guests.
... But this second wave with oxygen-cylinder shortages
death tolls and pipe-and-gas leakages sealed buildings and
floating bodies over rivers and patient peaks...
told me all the good and bad days had come
all together and at once.

And it was time to empty the anthill
to molt skin, for honey to erupt,
to really live.

αίμα

They are bursting on the streets
from a deep gash: wounds to capillaries
leaving the atriums and ventricles: vesicles of this city
that has closed gates on them.

They are hemorrhaging
after delivering their daily karma
of nutrients, oxygen to each cell
away and back from the city of vital substance.

They are releasing between (two) heartbeats –
a circulation of desperation: internal, external hematoma
drop-like footprints.

Feet sprouting bare earth
CO_2 releasing
from two vena cavas
as the city contracts its waste.

They are cleaning, carting it
away through tricuspid valves
they themselves disappearing
out on the cobalt street –

landless, nameless laborers
from a deep slash
of intracranial, intracerebral
big city-memory.

Note: A tribute to the exodus of migrant labor, who moved on foot from Mumbai to far away back home during the 2020 lockdown, some of whom never reached and many who did so under merciless circumstances.

Shadow Tilt

He sits with his eyes like sunken brown suns. '*I want to write like you – your poems*,' he says with stale admiration.

I ask him about Zeno's theory. I like that he knows nothing about it. Paraphrasing will not be guilt then.
Achilles and the tortoise with 15 miles between them and the earth rotating at even keel.
Achilles doesn't manage to reach or race the tortoise. Achilles doesn't even budge.
All in fixed position. Earth. Tortoise. Rotation.
Speed in strife and movement: in standstill.

In another tale, Achilles is one of the greatest warriors.
In another tale, the tortoise loses to a hare.
In yet another tale, the earth burns, or floods, or is subsumed by ice.

Achilles should be in search of himself, not the earth, not the tortoise. His reference points, a-changing.

new-age minimalism –
the Joneses downgrade
to nano vehicles

a penny for a scheme

Envy

When they die, they get precious.
Agha Shahid Ali.
Margaret Mascarenhas.

Because their sentences now have full stops
their muses have flown
or gone with them to Kashmiri-American poet graves
or Venezuelan-Goan ones.

Now their words have the weight of water and earth
sprinkled with burial tears.
These fireflies glow without extinguishing in the dark
permanent stars,
roses,
thorns.

Now nothing can be edited
everything, transient
temporary,
are the feelings of ever meeting them.

Now they are infused in the shape of clouds.
Permanent bookmarks
written in rock
smelted engravings in caves.

Now they fit into a frame
in the relationship of knowing a person by their biography on
Wikipedia,
where it won't need updating
every single day.

Their pictures will be limited
You can only go into the unknown past.

Now they have an original, unabridged word count
you can spell their names backward and still
reach their graves.

You don't have to say safe flights, safe journeys
– they are already home.

They are permanently watching you to see if you can
overdo their novels
their magnificent ghazals.

Can you startle their unblinking torchlit eyes
as they keep watching you?
Souls of tubelights
Souls of lampposts
Souls of engines of outstation trains that glide smooth.

They have a permanent question
you have temporary anthologies,
answers of story collections,
book launches going nowhere,
festivals.

They went into permanent print.
You are second and third reruns, reprints.

You are still being edited, W-I-P
hopelessly abandoned,
while they have a nice granite bedstead.

Viewfinder

(For Danish Siddiqui)

You should have returned
when your jeep was ambushed three days
before staring face with your killers
on the road to your Maker,
curating world occurrences and danger.

We know them theoretically.
They would have happened anyway
even if you didn't let six bullets
through your body like close range full-stops.

We would have known
the world is resurrecting,
half of it depleting:
one arm rising in hope
one arm stirring the muck.
Even if we didn't see it
in one more of your vivid photography:
the world kissing decadence
every minute
melting or rising phoenix-like
in a recursive cycle of seasons:
birth-and-death patterns.

Keeping its *hisaab-n-kitaab* of atrocities,
Profit&Loss statements of lives lost and lived.

You should have stayed
to shape golden moments with Sarah and Yonus.

If I were you, I would have chosen: the cowardice of sunlit
moments
to the blatancy of malignant cartridge.
No job should have the vacancy of death
making you choose thresholds. . .

and yet maybe Sarah and Yonus might have
learned a bigger lesson
in fearlessness and grit –
looking danger in the soul of a stark barrel gun.

That might have been moment enough
to jolt them into real existence.

Pulitzer Prize–winning Indian photo-journalist Danish was brutally killed by the Taliban in Afghanistan in 2021.

Abstruse

Light fell through one window
in a house, once
bending through thicket.

Rooms drowning in mirage-like silence,
its inhabitants seeing alphabet
debating in diverse languages
with visions turning rods and cones.

Rooms with lesser light had shadows flickering,
in the braille of gray
with books melting into roots
as ancient knowledge drew out superstition.
They held books upside down,
forming new letters and language.

Rooms in total darkness made from shapes of fantabulism.
Now inmates met
in the common room
(sometimes) as bedfellas.

Beings of Dark
lusted for fruit.

Clashes don't need vocabulary.

The Darkroom people used gibberish,
the Lightroom, polemics.

The dining room was in half light,
recording these mismatches
barbaric or warmup…?

As the Darkroom people amplified dread
the Lightroom people argued
over synonyms.
unease. terror. jolt. bogey.

Then one day
the Light itself retreated
leaving the mansion.

The people of Light couldn't go back to the Dark.
So the people of Dark inherited the whole house.

And this happened in every corner
of every earth.

The metamorphosis of the moth is
in the murmur of the flame.

Asynchronous

Everything's shut. See – we don't hear the churn of machine.
No grease in the cogs. No oil. The spare-parts shops are shuttered.
The decrepit post office at the edge of an unmapped town and the small roads leading out of it.
Even the postwoman's cycle lies like junk: tyres punctured, mirror broken.

Only two things have motion.

Zephyrus, who disembodies through his nostrils, armpits, mouth in *bhastrika pranayama*. And letters in creme envelopes, in calligraphic handwriting overflowing the red letterbox.
The letters pour in from the sky, cross-hairing dust-sun beams, splintering refraction.
Sometimes, the Universe, hurt and disillusioned, herself visits.
'Have you delivered my letter of 7th March?' she asks on 7th May.
As if these are not letters but water to wash streets of limbo; planks to build a ship to sail over an ocean of stars; plinths of new nations for houseboats and bamboo stilt-huts over lake soil; blueprints and iron rods to foster hot cement and concrete; dogmas of a new religion; bones for new skeleton.
Here are two more inlands. There, five. Fluttering mid-air to thin wind.

new earth –
ripe fruit
in jam, pickle, cheese

The Dogs of All Stories

They say if the dog got the bone
like the rabbit the carrot,
the story is over.

So the lame dog starts out on a dog's journey
over a road made barren minus-ing the rain,
... putting in a little storm.
Having a shapeshifter-traveller
in search of dog hide who
skins for leather
searches dog musk, tusk, teeth, paw,
fur and nail
to make ornaments for souks.

The dog always has to meet the traveller
in the plot point of the story of the road
and because the story cannot have one point of view
it must also carry the story of the wind
of rain, of pebble, and the dust that remains.

The traveller must take the dog on a digression,
the bone should shrink to half its size
or be eaten by rats, maggots, mites, and rodents.

The bone should be an ornament
on the Savage like a good-luck charm
or such an amok-thing...

The traveller must hypnotize the dog.
We must empathize with dog and traveller,
if we are true human beings.

To understand the traveller's psyche, you must understand his
wound.
He is not all that bad: just drifted, disoriented, demented
but of the same cell, bone, blood, corpuscle, tissue, marrow,
and soul.

The dog must save his life but lose his tail,
for one-eyed Odinian wisdom
and his tongue
but not his nose… to smell drift-wind
and come back on track,
limp on a journey through eternity.

The bone must move from the neck of the Savage after he is
killed –
the bone growing from him to new bone in an act of melding.

When the dog gets the bone or the bone gets the dog
it was the story of the bone all the way long
that we must realize we were pursuing.

Bedrock

We are given in to the roughness of the seas,
made to catch its erratic blue between our irises
taught of winds but not of sails
and never the ship.

Shipbuilding isn't a skill we learn since birth.
That is discovery.

The Bhagavad-gita is a logline,
its script in the fulcrum of its seed
the tree subverted –
growing through roots under
the surface of a psychic stampede.

For how is it possible for humanity,
to leave the gravity of labor
disconnecting it from fruit?

How can we train our fingers to sow seeds
but not chisel shaft, sheath, sickle, and scythe
for harvest and reap?

...sow seeds and let the rain decide when it came?
Balancing what we controlled and what we didn't?
Half of life spent confusing the two.
Most of life spent in controlling that
which we didn't control:

plan on executing the seas, cartographing tides,
calibrating plate shifts,
when our ships withered in its decks, sails, seams,
masts, 'n bodies?

And when we find the ship
after a long search through
a hard ocean
lying at the side of the shores, it is just the starting point.

To build it…
because it's the only ship we will ever have,
the only ship we will ever know.

Karm –
the labor of our palm lines.

Acknowledgements
it took a village to shape this poet

I thank my two international writing residencies – International Writing Program, University of Iowa (2015) and Charles Fellowship, University of Stirling (2017) – for instilling in me unprecedented levels of creative confidence. The literary and humane visionary Christopher Merrill for inviting me for three consecutive years as a creative-writing teacher to IWP's summer programs. Chetan Mahajan and the Himalayan Writing Retreat, and all the colleges and campuses that invited me to teach poetry. And my bright and crackling poet-colleagues of all ages and stages, whom I met along the way. Your spirit was so endearing, so enriching, I know what a forest of birdsong we have become! Your journey has inspired mine.

A special note of gratitude to my editor at Hachette India, Sonali Jindal, for being such an astute and passionate champion for this book.

My cheeriest gratitude to the jury of prizes and awards:
Norton Girault Literary Prize, UK 2018; Gregory O' Donoghue International Poetry Prize, Ireland 2018; Beverly Prize Poetry Book Award, UK 2019; 2nd Gaudy Boy Poetry Book Prize 2019, NY; Asian Cha's Auditory Cortex, 2018; The Great Indian Poetry Contest 2018; International Proverse Poetry Prize 2018; The RL Poetry India Award 2013; Wordweavers Contest, 2014; *Hourglass Literary Magazine*'s Poetry Award, 2016; Hungry Hill Competition in Ireland, 2017; David Burland Poetry Prize 2017; Rabindranath Tagore Literary Prize 2020.

My sincerest gratitude to the editors and publishers of anthologies: Poetry Foundation (editors: Kazim Ali and Rajiv Mohabir); the *Tampa Review* (ed.: Paul T. Corrigan); *Stand* Magazine, UK (ed.: Vahni Capildeo); the *Bloomsbury Book of Great Indian Love Poems* (ed.: Abhay K.); Best Asian Poetry 2021–22 anthology, Kitaab Singapore (ed.: Sudeep Sen); The Brown Boat; The *Finger* Magazine; Haibun Today; online journal *The Bamboo Hut*; *A Hundred Gourds*; Poems for the Road podcast (UK); *Zo Magazine*; bigbridge.in; poetryindia.com; bottle rocket; *The Dhauli Review*; *The Freshwater Review*; *The Daily Star*; the online poetry journal Kritya; *40 under 40: An Anthology of Post-Globalization Poetry*; the bilingual journal *Hakara*; *Veils, Halos & Shackles: International Poetry on the Oppression and Empowerment of Women*; *Joao-Roque Literary Journal*; Muse India; *Narrow Road* literary journal; *Café Dissensus* magazine; *The Punch Magazine; Chandrabhaga: A Magazine of Indian Writing*; *Verseville*; *Magazine* (ed.: Sonnet Mondal); *The Bombay Literary Magazine* (ed.: Pervin Saket); Sahitya Akademi's *Modern English Poetry by Younger Indians*; *The Shape of a Poem: The Red River Book of Contemporary Erotic Poetry*; *Converse: Contemporary English Poetry by Indians*, edited by Sudeep Sen, published by Pippa Rann Books & Media; *Yearbook of Indian Poetry in English 2021* (editors: Sukrita Paul Kumar, Vinita Agrawal), published by Hawakal Publishers; and Raza Foundation.

My heartfelt gratitude to the curators of festivals and stages that supported my poetry readings: Sahitya Akademi Delhi and Chandigarh, KalArt, Kala Ghoda Arts Festival, 100Thousand Poets for Change, Kitab Khana, Poetry Couture, Words Tell Stories, The Poetry Club, Women Empowered-India, Max

Mueller Bhavan, Crossover Poems, Goa Arts and Literature Festival, Institute Menezes Braganza, Hyderabad Literary Festival, Writer's Carnival, Caesurae International Conferences, Prakriti Poetry Festival, American Library, Bengaluru Poetry Festival, Hongkong's Out Loud, Fringe Club and Peel Street Poets, Iowa's Book Festival, Asia Pacific Writers and Translators (APWT), Lviv's International Literature Festival Ukraine, Hungary's FISZ20 Literary Camp, Gold Coast's Griffith University, Odisha Arts and Literature Festival, Vagdevi Literature Festival, Glass House Festival, Jaipur Literature Festival 2020, Shoolini Literature Festival, Emirates Literature Festival, Mathrubhumi International Festival of Letters, Yuvadhara Literature Festival, and Chitkara Literature Festival.

My earlier publishers: Paperwall Publishing (Hemant and Smruti Divate) and Copper Coin Publishing (Sarabjeet Garcha).

My creative partners and associates: The US Consulate General Mumbai – Dosti House, American Library, and the faculty of Wilson College and St. Xavier's College, Mumbai.

Thanking Philippa Collie Cousins and the Visible Poetry Project, and Shonda Rhimes' Shondaland for celebrating my poetry film, *Skirt*. And the late poet Jayanta Mahapatra, also a beloved mentor, and Philip Schultz, Adam Aitken, Patrick Cotter, Sandra Alcosser, and Luisa A. Igloria – poets I admire – for endorsing this published collection with their incisive eye and generous praise.

My loving family. My fellow-poets. My readers.